A BRIEF MOMENT IN TIME

A TRUE STORY

DR. RICHARD HAGEDORN

Author's Tranquility Press
ATLANTA, GEORGIA

Copyright © 2023 by DR. RICHARD HAGEDORN

All rights reserved. No part of this publication may be reproduced, distributed or transmitted in any form or by any means, including photocopying, recording, or other electronic or mechanical methods, without the prior written permission of the publisher, except in the case of brief quotations embodied in critical reviews and certain other noncommercial uses permitted by copyright law. For permission requests, write to the publisher, addressed "Attention: Permissions Coordinator," at the address below.

DR. RICHARD HAGEDORN/Author's Tranquility Press
3800 Camp Creek Pkwy SW Bldg. 1400-116 #1255
Atlanta, GA 30331, USA
www.authorstranquilitypress.com

Ordering Information:
Quantity sales. Special discounts are available on quantity purchases by corporations, associations, and others. For details, contact the "Special Sales Department" at the address above.

A BRIEF MOMENT IN TIME: A TRUE STORY/DR. RICHARD HAGEDORN
Paperback: 978-1-961123-41-0
eBook: 978-1-961123-42-7

Contents

Prologue

It looked like I had just gone through a major rain storm. My clothing was drenched in sweat though, not rain. I was so thirsty and felt like I was going to fall under the weight I was carrying. I had finished the water in my canteen by 11:00 a.m., and now it was noon, and I was already very thirsty. I carried four canteens of water. Most others only carried two, and even the four were not enough for me. I guess I just needed more water than most of the others. I was beginning to wonder if others were having trouble too or was it just me. I looked around and saw that everyone was pretty much as exhausted as I was. I looked further over to the right and saw a Marine lying on the ground with a corpsman next to him. His legs were kicking through the air like he was running. He was frothing from the mouth, and his eyes were rolled back in his head. He had fallen from heat exhaustion. I had told all my men to take extra salt tabs that morning. I knew it was going to be hot. One of the men had said that he heard the radioman say it was one hundred thirteen degrees already and still climbing. Someone else said, "It's going to get worse," not good news. I took five tabs that morning, pretty much my limit and had trouble keeping them down. They usually made me very nauseous after taking them, but I knew it was necessary. I know some of the men did not take any, even pretending to take them but then not because of the nausea, and that was a big mistake in this heat. I felt sorry for them now. I did manage five though and thought I should take a couple more, but you can only take so many of those before your body throws them back up. Almost immediately, the stomach begins to churn.

I readjusted the heavy equipment I was carrying and continued, determined to make it. As I moved through the heat, at times, things started to spin in my head; the bright sun beat down. I went to that dark, cool spot in the back of my helmet that I knew in my mind. I had been there often. There, it was cool, safe, dark, and comfortable. I continued through the heat that was only getting worse, just as they had said. I said a prayer to God and asked him to help me make it. He did. God was my constant companion and the reason I am alive through all the battles. I prayed to him many, many times every day. And he always answered my prayers.

Horst Faas, Associated Press

Chapter 1

The Beginning

March 6, 1968, was a day to remember. It started very early in the morning at 03:30:00 exactly, and by 04:12:11, I was standing near the ramp, leading up through the tunnel, going up from the deep fortified bunker we were temporarily calling home. When I awoke, I said a prayer as I did every morning in Vietnam, but this morning I prayed harder. I knew that most of us would be dead before the sun set in the sky. The bunkers were very deep and could withstand a direct hit from the thousand pounders that the enemy fired at us. Thousand pounders are very big and would put a deep hole in the ground when they hit. The bunkers need to be deep and strong, or otherwise, a direct hit would kill everyone inside. Ours was deep, about thirty feet underground, covered with sheets of steel, and then piled with sandbags. Now I knew ours would withstand a direct hit. The day before at 4:00 p.m. (which was pretty much the daily standard; after they first hit Khe Sanh); they fired fifteen rounds from the north above the DMZ at our parameter. We were located next to Khe Sanh and officially designated A3. We often would stand outside and watch them land on Khe Sanh; then go inside because we knew we were next. For the first time since we got there a week earlier, we received a direct hit on our bunker. The noise was deafening, and it filled the bunker with dust. We all held our breath waiting to see if it gave way, but it did not. So at least we knew we were safe down there. Safe down there but not when above ground, as we thought might happen later in the day. That was one of the reasons we were all nervous about what was going to happen today.

I was surrounded by boxes of hand grenades and ammo. I was handing out extra grenades to anyone who wanted some and as many as they wanted. After one of my men took three grenades, he lightly touched my arm before he started up the ramp to the outside. A few more men filed past then another touched my arm as he went. Next in line was my good friend Lance Corporal Murphy. I asked, "Why are these guys touching my arm?" He replied, "For good luck." And with that, he touched my arm and went up the ramp. I realized then that I had been lucky; I had not thought much about it before. I was probably the only one in the platoon who had seven months with the unit and had not been seriously wounded or killed. I did have my share of explosions under my belt, but to date, no serious wounds. I guess I was lucky. I sure did not feel that way though, and with what I knew about what was going to happen today, I did not know if my luck would hold. I also knew that it was not luck. You can only have so much luck and only so much skill. There was a lot more here going on, and I knew it. It was the constant prayer that was keeping me alive and also the idea that I would be the very best Marine I could be. That I would be good and honorable and take care of others the best I could, even in the middle of all this combat. This meant even treating the enemy with dignity and respect. There was an expression in Vietnam that I believed in very strongly and the other smart ones also accepted as law. That was the rule of payback, a simple rule. If you were mean or bad in some way, you would get payback, and it would take the form of the same kind of behavior. Things happened fast in war, a lifetime was lived in a matter of days, and justice was always delivered. Once a Marine said to me, "Oh, that guy is going to get payback." He was right. The Marine did get payback.

Did I believe this was God's work, or the hand of God? Yes. I believe this completely, 100 percent. I have no doubt. This, of course, did not happen to everyone who was injured or killed; most were simply natural acts in relationship to us doing our job. But sometimes we thought we saw payback at work.

One of the last men in the bunker, Private Jones, started by me but stopped suddenly and said, "Corporal Hagedorn, I am sure I will die today." This did startle me, and I thought, and I knew, many of us were about to die. I knew that half of us (of the two hundred fifty-four Marines in First Platoon, Charlie Company, First Regiment, First Marine Division), probably more, would be seriously wounded or killed before the day was over, and they knew too. We were going that day uphill, in the open, against fortified positions and in the range of the one thousand pounder guns deep in the hills of North Vietnam. These guns could be rolled out of there protective caves in the hillside and would unleash death upon us. At first, I did not know what to say to him then said, "What else can we do? We are Marines, and we must go. We really have no choice except to engage the enemy." I said this firmly as I looked directly into his eyes, which I could see were slightly clouded with tears. I felt so bad for him and wish I could have done something for him. I quickly thought maybe I could talk to a corpsman and get him out of this, but I knew a bad dream was not a good enough reason. I was really hoping I could give him strength. I was hoping I could give myself strength. I wanted to help him even if I could not help myself; I was scared too, very scared. Private Jones continued to look into my eyes for a second, then gave a slight nod and headed up the ramp. I never saw him again. He died that day with so many others, in that country so far away from our home.

I looked around as the last few men filed up the ramp. I wondered if I would ever see this place again. I was not sure. I prayed again and walked up the ramp.

March 6, 1968, 04:49:05

It was a cool morning as I came into the night sky from the bunker, but I knew it was going to get much hotter as soon as the sun came up. There was no moon, but the sky was clear, and the stars were very bright. It looked like the heavens were right on top of us; it was so bright. I do not remember it being this bright before. I wondered if it was a sort of sign.

I had four full canteens on my cartridge belt as usual. For some reason, I always got so thirsty. We were doing the final preparations before leaving the secured perimeter. I told everyone to take salt tabs; there were grumbles. No one wanted to take those. Next, I had a Marine jump up and down a couple times. He rattled too much. I pointed out where he needed to secure some items, a grenade banging against another, his canteen not tight in its pocket. I told everyone to make sure all their equipment was "quiet." It looked a little funny as everyone "buddied" up, and one would jump for the other. After a few minutes of this, we could jump up and down, and no one made any noise. That was very good as sound seemed to travel a long way at night, making it possible for the enemy to know we were on the way. Not that we really thought that they did not know we were coming once we went out the perimeter. They always seemed to know, and we knew they were watching all the time. As I was getting my men ready, the lieutenant passed by and informed us that first platoon would be point for the company and then indicated first squad would be point for the platoon. The first squad leader appointed a fire team to start off, fire team 1. I assigned myself and my best machine gun team to move with the first squad as direct support. Our machine guns were used as the focal point for both offensive and defensive action. I had heard somewhere that this was styled of the German tactical operations in World War II as regards the deployment of guns and troopers in a company. I do not know if that was true or not, but I know it worked well for the Marines in combat operations. The only problem was that it put me and my guns right in the middle of all the fire, every time. However, that was what I wanted. At least for me, I wanted that. I wanted very much to meet the enemy. My gun teams wanted that too. We were ready and eager to do our job as Marine gunners, but that does not mean that we were all at least a little afraid.

One of the new privates was appointed to be first on point, closely backed up by a more experienced Marine. This is how we did it. One of the brand-new guys (BNGs) always made a point. At first, I thought this was not fair and had even protested at one point. It was pointed out to me by one of the more experienced noncommissioned officers (NCO) that first, they need to learn, even if it did get them killed, and second, we could not afford to lose an experienced man as they were few and far between. We need to keep the experienced Marines alive so they can fight and train the BNGs as they come in. That did make sense, but I still felt sorry for the BNG who had to walk point that morning. I knew he would be the first to fall. Turns out, I was not quite right; he was the second. We filed out one by one, into the night, hoping the enemy was not watching but knowing they were. They were always watching.

I was happy to hear how quiet we were. For such a large body of men, complete with machine guns and mortars, hardly a sound could be heard in the darkness. Clouds had moved in very fast and had made it so dark that we could not even see the man in front of us. The order was passed that we should go single file holding the man's pack in front of us. This made going forward very slow for the next hour, but we gradually made progress. We snaked out of the perimeter and on down to the rice paddies surrounding our defensive area. As we passed the last rolls of barbed wire surrounding the position, we all quietly locked and loaded our weapons. Now we were ready to fight. That moment always gave me a sense of excitement. I could feel the blood coursing in my body, the excitement of the impending battle. I could feel the excitement all around me; it did seem a little strange, but a lot of things did not make a lot of sense in those days. Many times, it was not logic that prevailed, but just feeling, emotions of the moment. I was getting used to that now.

Often it was difficult to make contact with the enemy. They usually would only fight when they had a clear advantage in terms of terrain or a strong ambush position and then often only making brief contact to inflict as much damage as possible, then breaking and running, leaving one man behind as a holding action and to ultimately die as we closed in. This man was always a senior noncommissioned officer (NCO) and was always difficult to kill because they were senior a sergeant. He would always fight until we killed him. I did respect that bravery and dedication to his comrades, and that technique worked well for them, allowing the main body to fade into the jungle. That was very frustrating to us as we might have several dead Marines before we got him, and we really wanted to even the score a little.

They would engage in combat when we would have trouble maneuvering, such as around water, dense jungle, or steep hills. I already knew where I was going to meet him today. It was going to be on a very steep hill that still had dead Marines on it from the two previous days of fighting. "A" company had "gone up" two days ago. We could hear the intense fighting going on from our perimeter. We had heard that they only made it part way up. The next day, Bravo Company assaulted. They had made it a little further up and brought back most of the dead Marines from A Company but had left some of their own out there. Our job today would be to take the hill plus bring back all of Alpha and Bravo Companies dead plus any we had. No one wanted to go up a fourth time, so we wanted to complete this today. Additionally, we wanted this done because they had set up such a large force so close to us, pretty much within a mile or so of our base perimeter. We could not allow them to stay there. We had to take back the lands around us and especially that hill or face even more damage, as they could then establish a base to attack our main perimeter from.

I let my mind wander a little and was thinking about the events on the first of January and Christmas. Christmas was lonely. It was the first time I was away from home and did not celebrate it. There was nothing special about Christmas Eve or Christmas Day, just the events as usual. On New Year's Eve, I decided I would do something a little different. I decided that I would go outside the perimeter to buy a bottle of whiskey and drink it for New Years. Where we happened to be was a little further south of the DMZ, and we were actually right next to a small village. I knew this was completely against the rules, but a good Marine does break the rules once in a while. Schweitzer (more about Schweitzer a little later) always told me I was too much of a goody-goody Marine, and that I needed to toughen up a little. Get a few glitches on my record. So, I am determined to do this after dark. I went to my squad and asked if anyone was willing to come with me. I really did not want to go alone. One guy volunteered. He was new and interested in adventure. We walked to the main gate just after dark. I had a pistol, and he carried a rifle but no other gear. It was a nice evening. We stopped at the gate, and I told the guys on guard there what we were going to do. I told them we would whistle when we came back and confirmed the challenge and password. They opened the barbed wire, and we headed into the village. It was dark, no lights just a few candles burning in the huts of the villagers. We came to the first hut, and we knocked on the door. The owner answered, and through some sign language, I asked who would sell whiskey. He directed me to a village hut where he said I could get it. I knocked on the door, and a nice middle-aged woman answered the door. She invited us into her home and closed the door. The hut was one room with beds in the corner. She had a cooking area and an area for worship with the Holy Cross and a small statue of Mother Mary. She also had two daughters about ten and twelve years old who sat on the bed playing with dolls. They smiled at us. I hoped they were not afraid of us with our weapons and all. We smiled at them and said hi. The hut had a dirty floor, but the mother and children looked very clean, and the hut was very neat. I asked in English if she had whiskey, and she nodded yes and went behind a box in the kitchen area and brought out a bottle of silver Fox whiskey. I had heard about this and been told not to drink it because it could cause you to go blind. I did not really believe that but was concerned anyway. I asked if she had something else, and she said no so I decided to take it. Then I realized I had no money. I had gotten so used to not using money I did not even think about it. The Marine with me did not have any either. The lady was so nice. She told me to take it anyway. I felt bad and promised her I would bring her the money the next night. She smiled and shook her head yes. We said goodbye to her and the girls and headed back to the perimeter. When we got close to the gate, I whistled and answered the challenge word, and we were back, safe inside. I was just settling down to enjoy my Silver Fox when the radioman came up and said he was looking for me; there was a squad leader meeting going on at the Platoon CP. I grabbed my helmet and headed for the CP. The meeting was already in progress, and the lieutenant gave me a quick look as I entered but said nothing to me and just continued with the briefing. He was talking about a pull out early in the morning to go and help a company that was being overrun as we were being briefed. We were to relieve them and take over their perimeter as they were suffering high casualties (this was the march I was talking about in the prologue). As he talked, I was thinking that we would not be here tomorrow night and how could I pay for the whiskey? I decided I would go back that night and take care of my obligation. The lieutenant dismissed us, and I went back to my squad to hold a squad meeting. They knew something was up and were eager to hear what. I told them the situation and then asked for a volunteer to come back with me to the village. The guy who went with me before was not really interested, but one of my other guys said he would go just to make sure I was OK. That was nice of him; I know he did not really want to go. Also, I had to borrow money from the men because I did not have any. They gave me a bunch of Piasters, the designated money in Vietnam at that time. We were not allowed to carry American money. I wondered where they got this but did not ask. We walked to the gate. The Marine with me did not carry a rifle. I asked him about that, and he said, "I won't need it." I did take my pistol, and I was pretty sure we would not need weapons on this trip. We stopped at the gate, and I made the same deal with the same guys before we went out. We were able to quickly find the hut, and I knocked gently to not alarm the lady and her children. She answered the door right away and let us in. The girls were in bed but not asleep yet. They giggled and said something in Vietnamese that I did not understand. I smiled and said, "Hi there." I gave the mamasan all the money, and she was very grateful. I probably overpaid her but did not know the cost and did not know the value of the money I gave her. I didn't really care either. Money was not of a lot of value to us. I could not tell her we were leaving in the morning, and that was why we were back so soon, but I think she may have thought we would be right back anyway, so I was very glad we came back to pay her. We said good night and left heading directly back to the gate. When we were about twenty meters from the gate, I gave my whistle, but there was no response from the gate. I tried again. Still no response; I was getting nervous, and the Marine with me looked scared. It was very dark, but we were close enough I could see his face. I was thinking, *Shit, I hope I don't get both of us killed over a bottle of whiskey.* Then we heard the thump close to us. We both thought at the same moment, *Grenade!* We went down to the ground and waited for the explosion. I was wondering if American grenades where more deadly than Chinese. I thought so. I waited for the explosion. In the distance, a flare went off, so we had a little light, and I was thinking about waving at the gate but thought that would not do much good and might get us shot in the dim light from the flare. Then we heard another thump. I said, "Oh, shit." Aloud this time. The Marine next to me said, "It's a rock!" I said, "What!" He said, "A rock! They are just trying to scare us." I thought, but did not say, *well, it worked.* We got up and went to the gate. As we approached, we could hear their laughter. As we walked by, I said, "Asshole!" but with a good-natured smile; they continued to laugh as we walked back to our bunkers. It was funny though, at least today, not so funny that night. I settled down to enjoy my prize. I offered the Marines who went with me, but they declined so I found a quiet spot at the end of the trench line in an empty bunker, sat back, relaxed, and looked out the bunker parapet at the "natural" fireworks of Vietnam on New Year's Eve. I enjoyed about one-third of the bottle. This was my only time slightly intoxicated in Vietnam. At 1:00 a.m., I gave the bottle to the rest of the squad and went to bed wishing everyone a Happy New Year. I knew we had an early morning wakeup, so I wanted to sleep off the whiskey a little. In the morning, we boarded trucks to take our part way to the besieged Marine company; the rest we would walk. As the trucks pulled out, we passed near the hut where I had purchased the whiskey last night. All of a sudden, the door opens up, and the mamasan and her daughters came running out. They ran right for the trucks, and I could see them frantically looking over the men in the trucks. They continued to chase the trucks, running alongside. I knew they had come to say goodbye to me. I thought about hiding behind my helmet but decided to let them see me. They did and started waving at me, smiling and speaking excitedly in Vietnamese. I smiled and gave a wave goodbye to them. They were so happy, and they started jumping up and down continuing to wave as we pulled out of sight. The men looked at each other; not understanding what was going on and looked at me with puzzled looks. I saw Lieutenant Hawkins give me a long look too, but he never said anything to me. I sat back in the truck and was very happy. Someone actually saying goodbye to me; some of the people we were really fighting for! It was a great day, and I felt so good. This was my one and only encounter with Vietnamese civilians, and it was a very good one. I was very happy.

We had navigated through the rice paddies separating the two hills without incident, and we were nearing the base of the "enemy" hill. I like the night. It seemed safer to me. At first, when I got to Vietnam, I did not like it as I could not see the enemy, and there were so many night sounds, but gradually I got use to that and began to realize there was real protection in the darkness. At first, I wanted to always see a flare in the sky, lighting up the area around us. There usually was funny how they kept them going non-stop through the night. As soon as the last one started to touch the ground, another would go off. I would sit through my watch at night and watch them slowly drift down on their parachute. I kept expecting the mortar team to miss a beat and then we would have total darkness. I would wait to watch, wondering if it would be this time. It never was. They would just silently drift down, one after another, without end. At first, for me this was great, but gradually I learned to appreciate the dark. It seemed that we had a better advantage than the enemy at night. If you did not fire your weapon and relied primarily on grenades, the enemy could not tell where you were at. They usually attacked at night, and I found that the darkness was my friend. As they would move in on us, sooner or later, they would have to fire and that would give away their position. Then we could unleash our fire power into them. After a few hours of slow moment, the horizon began to light up slightly as the sun began to rise. We gradually could make out a few more details in the darkness. As it got lighter, we spread out the formation. "Bunching" up was taboo. If one of us stepped on a land mine, it might take out many of us at a time. And then it happened. One of the Marines to my right rear from the first squad stepped on a mine.

I fell to the ground and rolled, coming up with my weapon aimed in the direction of the explosion, ready to fire. I saw a Marine floating in the air among a cloud of debris and smoke. He rose, almost in slow motion into the sky, about forty feet, and then fell back to the earth. Someone yelled for a corpsman. There was a lot of yelling. I could hear the Marine moaning in pain. He was in very bad shape. The corpsmen were surprised he was still alive. I was too. Three of them worked on him for nearly an hour to stop the bleeding. Both of his legs were gone above the knee, one arm was gone, and the other was intact but only had two fingers left on the hand. They said the parts were completely disintegrated with no trace of them left. A medevac helicopter was brought in finally, and the Marine rewash moved to the hospital in Da Nang then on to Japan. We heard he survived; I was surprised, and with the aid of a nurse, he sent us a postcard about a month later. He wished us all the best and said that he was recuperating. For him the war was over, and I felt very sad for him.

March 6, 1968, 08:31:10

We continued with our "attack." Any element of surprise was definitely gone now. But few of us thought there was a surprise element even from the beginning. We moved forward in battle formation. I was watching the point man. He was about fifty feet in front of us; far enough but still close enough so we could see him. He had just given a signal to hold up. He was looking intently directly in front of him, about thirty feet away, at a clump of bushes beneath a cluster of trees. The squad leader behind him squatted down and held up his hand in a closed fist gesture to signal a halt. All men began to crouch, but before we were completely down, I saw the point man start to crumble to the ground. Almost immediately, I heard the round bang through the air as the sound reached us; it was the sound of an AK47. I then went into my standard to the ground, rolled, and immediately lit a fire on the bush area, emptying a full clip into it. I ejected the clip and with one smooth motion as the clip ejected reached down to my pouch on my cartage belt and grabbed a second clip. This I did, and I was going to complete one more roll, all part of my standard procedure when if I was directly fired on. I did this without thinking and was always part of my plan, unless I was in a spot where I could not roll, like the time on the cliff ledge. The idea was to get to the ground as fast as possible and, while going down and still falling, empty a clip on the enemy position. This was my own technique, not something taught in training, and was a process I used whenever we were ambushed (which did happen on a regular basis). I liked emptying the clip as I went to the ground. It gave me the feeling of immediate response and helped to try and establish "fire superiority" over the enemy. That was important, especially if they had you in an ambush. You need to get control of the situation by firing back more bullets than they were firing at you. That is fire superiority. On landing, as I rolled, I would eject the first clip, reach down and get a second, insert it, finish the roll coming up into the firing position, and empty a second clip on the enemy. Finally, I would do one more roll, ejecting the second clip, inserting a third clip and coming to a firing position but this time, hold fire, and determine what to do next. It was important to get fire superiority, but we had to also watch the number of bullets we fired. We only carried so many, and it seemed there were never enough. I had decided early on to carry two extra clips beyond the recommended number just for this purpose. As I felt and fired the first clip, a round from the enemy landed just in front of me. It threw dirt into my face. I completed the second role. I emptied the second clip directly into the bush. I decided to do two rolls this time to get out of the area a little more before taking up the firing position and also considered firing a third clip. I had decided to fire another clip when I heard the "ploop, ploop" as the two grenade men from squads 1 and 2 began returning fire on the clump of brush. Using the M79 grenade launchers, the grenadiers sent several rounds of HEAT into the brush. After that, the bush was silent. I saved my third clip. A corpsman rushed to the downed point Marine. He was dead. Hit right in the face by the round, and there was not much of his face left. The rounds from the AK47 are large in caliber. This makes the weapon effective over long distance and in close range; it can do a lot of damage to the human body. We moved then into the brush area where the firing had come from. One North Vietnamese Army Regular (NVA), NCO, laid dead, his uniform ripped apart by the blasts from the grenade launchers, and he had several bullet holes in his chest. I hoped some of those were mine. One of the Marines secured his AK47, and we moved on, up the base of the hill. We moved out in full formation with a new point man designated and flanking fire teams. I again was up with the point squad, just behind the squad leader. I had my two machine guns spread out on either side of me, ready to deploy immediately.

Up the Hill, 10:28:15

Now we began to move up the hill. The first platoon was now in the center and the primary point unit with first and second squads moving together and third being held in reserve behind us. There were two other infantry platoons in the company, and the second platoon would move up the hill on our right with third platoon on our left. The company was a reinforced company; meaning it was made up of three infantry platoons and a fourth platoon that was the weapons platoon. I was a member of the weapons platoon. In the weapons platoon, there were three machine gun squads of which I was in and lead the first squad. I was detached to the first infantry platoon with my two guns, each of the three infantry platoons got one gun squad with two guns in it. In the weapons platoon, there were also M60 mortars and bazooka/flame thrower men. These stayed with the weapons platoon and were not detached to the infantry platoons as the gun squads did. Finally, there were the company command personnel, such as company radiomen, messengers, etc., along with the detached corpsmen who were not Marines at all but actually navy men. Of course, technically, the Marines were part of the navy too, but we were not actually called navy. This all sounds a little complicated but is just basically a three-tier system. All these men put together totaled two hundred fifty-four making up the attack that day.

It was getting hot fast, already at ninety-five degrees. It was a steep hill and littered with the debris from the two previous battles on it. The fact that the dead sniper was NVA gave me a lot of information. His equipment looked to be in good condition (other than torn apart by our attack). This indicated that his unit was probably well trained and supplied. Many of those we had previously fought did not have much in the way of equipment. They were usually easier to kill or would run after an initial contact. Also, they were not typically good shots. This unit looked like it would hold and fight to the end, and they did.

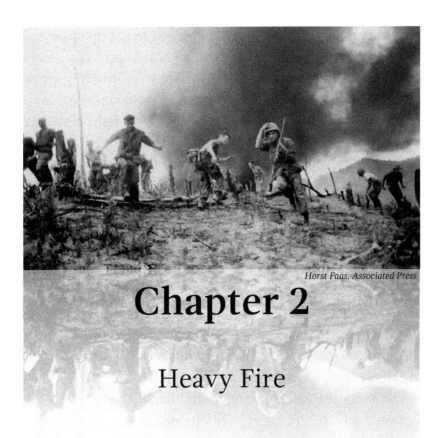

Horst Faas, Associated Press

Chapter 2

Heavy Fire

We started taking heavy fire almost right away. The first squad was in front of me and my guns, so we had to be careful where we fired. I could not make use of the machine gun as there was not a good field of fire as we moved up. Additionally, in a situation like this, you did not want to expose your guns as they would have been a primary target for the enemy. It was necessary to keep them quiet for the right time, and then they could be used to their full power. The enemy had the tactical advantage over us. They were in fortified positions and dug in. Many had covered, sandbagged tops; meaning it was difficult to toss in a grenade, get a hit with mortar or M79 grenade launcher. For those, we needed to get up close and toss in a grenade or get a flame thrower in there. They were set up to maximize their fields of fire with crossing fields and the ability for one position to protect another. That meant, as we moved in and took out one fight hole, we would be getting fired on by another. We were on open ground, completely exposed and easy targets. Several first squad Marines were already down as the enemy fired from their positions. Once in a while, one would "pop up" and give us a clear shot, which we took. I did not understand why they did this as they were so safe down behind their sandbags. I think they just got excited when they saw a lot of clear shots and would stand and fire. We took advantage of the opportunity. The Marines ahead of us were firing and throwing grenades as they advanced, which helped a little. The explosions helped to prevent our movement up the hill to some degree. I yelled up to the squad leader for his men to use some smoke. He nodded and had his men threw out a couple smoke grenades. This helped a lot more. I used smoke a lot, not only to attack a position but also to obscure our position. Sometimes, if my machine gun position was taking fire, I would toss out smoke grenades in front of us so the enemy could not see exactly where we were. I used this also when we would move from the primary position to the secondary position as that would obscure our movement and the enemy would not know that we moved position. They would usually continue to fire through the smoke, and we would hear the bullets whizzing by but at least they did not have a direct target to aim at. If there was a hit, it was more or less a lucky hit. This gave us some comfort in knowing that it would be more or less a random shot that got us rather than an aimed round, but then I thought we would be just as dead either way. I know; however, this did help to reduce casualties. I thought of smoke like darkness. I liked the night because we could move without being seen, and smoke served the same purpose during the day. And sometimes we even used smoke at night. If there were a lot of parachute flares floating down as there usually were during any of our attacks or if we were attacked at night, then the smoke could still serve as a protective screen to hide us from the enemy. I never did see the enemy use smoke, and I wondered why. If they attacked and were in the open, they had no cover at all. The fact that we could use smoke when we needed it and that the enemy did not have it gave us a great advantage, I think.

The enemy continued to rake us with fire, but instead of a clear shot, they were only hitting us occasionally with a lucky shot through the smoke. With this technique, we were able to close in the enemy bunkers. We had flame throwers with my weapons platoon. I "called them up," and we got them close enough to use against the enemy in some of the bunkers. To get them close enough though, there needed to be some support. We had to get them there "safely." This was difficult given the intense fire from the enemy and would have been impossible without the smoke, but we were successful. Also, from the rifle squads, the M79 grenade launchers kept a barrage on the enemy bunkers as the Marine's grenadiers moved fired, reloaded, and fired again. I saw many direct hits from the grenadiers. I saw a few occasions where the bunkers were covered, and the grenadiers were able to put the HEAT round right through the front window. How was that for a special delivery?

They were very good, and one hit would usually silence the position. We did not have mortar or artillery support and I wondered why. Perhaps the lieutenant thought we would be moving too fast for that, at least with the mortars as they were directly attached to us. I wished for just one Marine jet to stream over and drop his payload of HEAT or napalm right in front of us as they had done on many other occasions. Once, in particular, the napalm was so close the heat scorched the tops of our helmets as we lay face down, hoping he would not miss and incinerate us. I heard later that March 6, 1968, was a busy day, and many other battles were under way that day. There was another Marine unit fighting for its life nearer to the Gulf of Tonkin. They were getting most of the artillery and air support including thousand pounders from the USS *New Jersey*, just off the coast.

We continued to move but were taking a lot of casualties now. With smoke, we got to the next bunker and took it out with grenades. I saw the squad leader from the first squad fall along with another Marine next to him. This fire was from another bunker position directly in front of us. We moved on that position. I threw one grenade then another as we closed the distance. One of my assistant gunners was able to flank it and get a grenade into it but was immediately shot from somewhere to our right. I could not get a clear view of that enemy position as some of the smoke obscured my view. The smoke worked for us and sometimes against us. However, we were able to get to the bunker. As the last of the first squad fell, the platoon lieutenant behind me ordered the second squad to take point. He had me hold my machine guns up, while the second squad maneuvered in front of us. We were eager to move up, but I followed orders and moved my men in a line. A little to the right of our main attachment, in a little denser brush; I got them down, placing the guns about fifteen feet on either side of me. So far, I had only lost one man, my assistant gunner from my primary gun. I heard a lot of firing further out on our right flank, and the radioman with the lieutenant said as he passed by me, "It is the second platoon attacking on the right flank." It sounded like they were pretty much even with us in going up the hill and about one hundred meters to our right. I was glad they were out there covering that flank. In the brush in front of us, about sixty feet away, I heard and saw some movement but nothing clearly. Then there was a burst of AK47 fire from that direction. Rounds struck in front of our impromptu line. We were close enough to them, within grenade range. Rather than fire and give away our exact position, I tossed a grenade. I was told a little later by the gunner to the right of me that had a clear shot at the enemy and just as he was about to fire the grenade that I threw had hit the enemy right in the center of his chest and as it flew away it immediately exploded. He did not need to take his shot.

Our grenades had roughly a thirteen—to fourteen-second delay on them, so I made it a practice to pull the pin and let the spoon fly. This would start the thirteen-second count before the explosion. Depending on the distance to the enemy, I counted to between seven and ten before I threw. This usually always made the Marine in the hole with me very nervous. If I dropped the grenade by mistake, we would have been dead. The value of this approach though was that it gave the enemy no chance to grab it and throw it back at us, which they would do if they could. If they did get it back to the Marine, there was never time for a third go-round (well usually not). I am sure that many of them reached for my grenade, thinking they had time left like with most of them (since no one else that I ever met would hold a live grenade and then throw like I did), and just about when they got hold of it, it went off. It was dangerous to hold on to them like this, but I thought it was worth the risk. Not one grenade that I threw out was ever returned, and I threw a lot of grenades, all told I would say over five hundred. Not all these five hundred were aimed directly at an enemy. Sometimes, especially in the dark, if I heard any noise, I would toss one out. Sometimes, just at random, noise or not, I would toss one just in case someone very silent was moving in my direction and their zappers could be very quiet. In fact, the expression was that if we were in perimeter and firing start from a night attack, you could be sure that zappers with satchel charges were already inside ready to toss those charges in any bunkers they found. They usually found the bunkers from the rifle and machine gunfire coming from them. They would just pull the pin on their satchel charges like grenades and toss them in, then run like hell. In the confusion with all the firing going on, they did not need to crawl back out. They would run out after being as destructive as they could be, while their infantry troops would pour in through the gaps created by the zappers. I was told when I got to Vietnam that if I was in a perimeter that was attacked, I could count on the fact that they were already inside and that each fox hole had to become its own fighting position, not to rely on the fact that there were still Marines in the hole next to you. They said, "You are on your own if they attack you at night."

That is why I told my gunners to use grenades first if we are attacked at night. Don't fire either guns or rifles until things are going for a while. The zappers would usually toss the explosives within the first few minutes and then try to get out before we could kill them. The grenade was my weapon of choice in a defensive position, especially at night and especially when being attacked at night.

As I said, holding the live grenade until the count of seven (I actually always used seven and no other number, except once in a while I would go to ten to get the aerial effect; I thought that was lucky, even though that was half way to fourteen, still, you had to pick some number), this was not a technique recommended in boot camp or training, and I am sure would be frown upon by the Marine trainers, but one I used and as I indicated, I preferred to do this when I was alone in a hole and did not endanger any other Marines. I do not recommend this to anyone else, and I know that some of you reading this book will be in combat and will consider this. If you do, be alone when you do this (if you are alone, then no one knows you are doing it and only you can be injured, I mean killed), and be very, very careful.

One of my guys told how he threw the grenade right away, the way we were taught, letting the spoon fly as we tossed the grenade. The enemy picked it up and threw it back right into their fox hole, he then picked it up, and threw it back a final time at which point it exploded immediately. I said smiling, "You really should do it my way," although I really did not advocate this approach. He answered, "Hell, I don't know about that." As I said, most did not like the idea of holding a live grenade, and I do not blame them. These things were known to have a "short fuse" (especially the old Korean

War pineapple grenades) and could go off in as short a time has five or six seconds. If you are counting to seven or really pushing it, and going for ten, you may not make it. I thought about it and decided the risk was worth the benefit, and I tried to be alone when I did this so I would not injure anyone else with this dangerous maneuver if something went wrong. The ones I was using this day were the new "baseball" grenades, which appeared to be much more reliable in terms of fuses and reliability of going off. When I first got to Nam, we were using the "pineapple" grenades left over from the Korean War (and eating their c rations too, which did taste old); evidently there was a surplus left from that war. And we needed to use those up first, even though they were not always reliable.

The enemy did not expect me to do this, and it was dangerous but very effective. I often wondered and pictured the enemy reaching for one of my grenades thinking he had plenty of time left and have it explode just as he got it. Also, in a brush like we were in, if I waited a few extra seconds, I could get the grenade to go off in the air, right over the enemy. This increased the chance of creating more casualties on their side from an "air burst" effect. I agree that it was a bit of a dangerous game, but it was an effective one, and that is what we were there for. It was not supposed to be safe, and we were there to kill the enemy, as many as we could, with as few casualties to ourselves as possible.

We continued to advance as the second squad took the lead and into the fire. I maneuvered my squad right behind second squad and this time right behind the lieutenant and his radioman. I suspected the third squad was being held in reserve for the final push. I was wondering how my best friend Corporal Hall was doing. He was my best friend and the leader of the third squad. We became friends, as best you can as we were not allowed to talk much, in boot camp. We then went to the Infantry Training Regiment (ITR) together. There I was selected to go into machine guns, and he went to the regular infantry training. We were both sent to Hawaii for amphibious training for ten months with the Twenty-sixth Marine Expeditionary Force at Kaniowii Bay before we were both given orders to Vietnam. We then both wound up in the same platoon, First Platoon Charlie Company, First Marine Division, in the Quang Tri province along the Demilitarized Zone (DMZ) in Vietnam. Hall was the nicest man I had ever met and, even at this late date, still holds that distinction. He was a good, caring person and the best Marine I have ever met. At first in Vietnam, we had spent many nights sharing a fox hole, getting to know each other better and better, before we took over our squads in the first platoon. On my first night in Nam, we were in a hole together on the northern perimeter of Da Nang. The perimeter got "hit" by mortars and sappers right in front of us. The way it happened it was raining, and a poncho was spread over the top of the hole by its previous owners. There was water in the bottom of the hole, so I was asleep on the sand bags on the top of the back of the fox hole. I was suddenly awakened by a hand pulling me into the hole, right into the mud on the bottom of the whole, face first. As I hit the mud, there was a loud explosion and a big flash of light. I remember I was mad at being awakened so unceremoniously and dumped into the water and mud, but then I realized what was going on. A mortar round landed right behind where I was laying. Mortars continued for about fifteen minutes, racking up and down the line of fox holes with some mortars making direct hits on the positions, killing the men in the hole. We had several close calls but not a direct hit. In the morning, we could see the poncho was riddled with holes from that first mortar. Hall had saved my life.

We were about halfway up the hill now I guessed. It looked like we were going to make it, maybe, but I knew we had a lot left to get through. I heard that they had heavy machine guns near the top, and mortars—oh yes, the mortars, and just at that moment the enemy mortars started. They were hitting right along the line of the advancing second squad. The rifle fire had let up, and we must have passed through the first of the fortified positions, one more to go and then the assault on the ridge line. A lot of men started falling and were being blown up from the mortars. This was bad as they continued to get chewed up. The fire was very accurate probably because of the two previous days of "practice" on us. We pushed on through the mortars, and they seemed to let up a little. About one-third of the second squad was lost at this point. I had one additional wounded, but he was still a field ready ammo-humper with a light wound to his right arm from shrapnel. A corpsman bandaged him up, and he was good as new. Wounds had to be very serious to actually take us out of action. We moved for about two hundred meters with no contact. We entered an open, flat area. This must have been where Bravo Company had made it too. There was left over debris from the previous day's battle. The blood on the ground looked fresh, and there were battle dressings laying everywhere. Equipment was strewn about, helmets, packs, and cloths but no weapons, no ammo, and more importantly no bodies. We were told that there were twelve Marines missing from the two previous days that we needed to locate, one from Alpha Company and eleven from Bravo. Bravo had managed to bring back many of the men from two days ago who were lost by Alpha, but they could not get them all, and I was about to find out why. At least for one dead Marine, the one I retrieved a little later in the day.

12:00:00

It was now one hundred eleven degrees. I was down to my last canteen of water already. I knew we still had a hot day in front of us, and there was no water to be had up here, as far as I could tell. Climbing the hill was difficult, and I was carrying about one hundred thirty-five pounds of weight, counting the extra grenades and ammo plus one extra canister of machine gun ammo. I was not alone; most of the men were completely out of water. The climb with the extra weight in the heat had caused everyone to go through their water very fast. We continued to move on and then the 50-caliber machine gun opened up on us. As I moved forward, I could hear the bullets going by me, and they were hitting the ground around me sending up small clouds of dust. I began wondering if I would be hit as I moved forward. Bullets were flying at me from everywhere, not just the 50 but lots of AK47 rounds were zipping by. I did not think I was going to make it the next ten steps, but somehow, I made it to a bomb crater. Two other Marines jumped in with me. I did not recognize them, but they must have been part of the second squad. One of them had one smoke left, and I threw it out as far as I could about twenty meters in front of the enemy 50 caliber. That got us close enough to throw another "smoke," which someone else did and then we were able to get the last fifteen meters, which was now close enough. The Marines immediately moved in and took out the position. We captured the 50, and now we had the 50, it was ours! I found two of my men to man it. We turned it around and opened it on the enemy. I smiled to myself as I thought about how surprised they must have been. Don't think they expected to have their own powerful weapon turned against them, and the 50 was powerful. The bullets were very large for this machine gun, and the gun itself was very heavy, not something you could carry through the jungle. Because of the size of the bullet, the rounds could travel a very great distance with accuracy. They were also very powerful and would mow right through trees and even rocks. I found out later that day that one of the Marines was climbing up the bunker position, in the smoke, to toss a grenade and one round from the 50 hit him right in the face. There was nothing left of his head. That was very sad and shocking; glad I did not know about it at the time. But we had the gun now! With the 50, we could reach easily to the crest of the hill. This gave us a tremendous fire power advantage. Fire power was what it was all about. Once we could get that, we could then take the enemy.

We could see the ridge line now; at least it looked like the ridge line. The 50 had a position to fire over our heads and right at the ridge, and there was at first a lot of fire coming from the ridge, but once we opened up on them, the fire diminished substantially. I found third platoon forward elements and asked them to take over the 50 as we began to move up again and this time without much resistance. It looked like we were going to make it now. Hawkins, our lieutenant, called us to a halt though for some reason. I am not sure why. The radioman came up to me and said: "Corporal Hagedorn, the lieutenant wants you to take your men over to the right flank and hold that area." He then took the lead, and we filed off to the right into an area pretty dense with jungle. This was not a scenario to deploy my machine guns in as there was no field of fire, meaning no open areas in front of us. I did not understand why Hawkins put us over there as it certainly was not a good area for machine guns. I told my men that for the time being, we were infantry, meaning no firing of the machine gun. With the jungle all around us, if we opened up with a machine gun, the enemy could easily move in and take it out with a few grenades. They loved to do that just as we did when their guns opened up. It was like a focal point; once you heard the gun, there was something that told you needed to take it out. I told my two gunners to under no circumstances open up. Here, the best weapons were the hand grenades; that way, the enemy could not determine our position easily. Of course, we could use our rifles and change position occasionally; this worked well also. It was important to always look around, a little bit to the right or left behind your current position and decide ahead of time where to fall back to if your position came under heavy fire. I felt the fallback position was critical to survival, especially at night. As we spread out a little, I found a hole made by artillery, which I jumped into with one of my men. It was a ready-made fox hole, no digging necessary. I noticed a small hill just to the left and back a few feet, that would be my fallback if necessary. I did not know how long we would be here, sometimes minutes, sometimes hours, and sometimes days, but I was ready. From my position, I had a little clearing in front of me of about nine meters. Just beyond that, there was a slight bank with perhaps a small road or trail behind it. There was a lot of firing going on around us but not right where we were at. That was nice, a brief vacation from the war. The primary firing was coming from our left flank, where we had just left. There was also fire coming from our right flank about fifty meters away. I figured that this must be the second platoon moving up. It sounded like they were a little ahead of us, but I was not sure. I wondered how they were doing, hoping that it was going ok for them. A lot of my hearing was gone because of the explosions and gunfire earlier, but I could still hear a little. In some battles, it was completely lost. I thought I heard something out in front of us to the right a little. I warned the Marine next to me and pointed in the direction I thought I heard it. We both got ready. I could see some brush moving, so I was certain someone was moving around out there. I thought about tossing a grenade but decided to wait. About a minute passed and then right in front of me and moving down the raven was an enemy soldier, NVA. He was semi crouched down as he moved. He looked straight ahead intently to my right. He did not see me and did not know I was there. I aimed in with my rifle. I could only see the top of his shoulders and his head. I took aim at the side of his head. For some reason I hesitated, I think because he was so young. He looked like he was only fourteen or fifteen years old, seemed so young to die. Then I thought, well I am just twenty, not all that much older. Seemed funny how kids were playing real grownup life and death games. I waited a little longer. I do not know why I was hesitating, but I think it was because he did look so young, and I am sure he could feel me watching him. I had had those same feelings and could tell when I was being watched. He slowly turned his head in my direction and saw me. I fired; his helmet flew off as he went down behind the bank. I immediately reached for a grenade because I was not absolutely sure I had gotten him, plus I thought there were probably more behind him. I pulled the pin let the spoon fly and waited six seconds then threw the grenade. It went off just as it cleared the other side of the bank. If the bullet missed, I was pretty sure the grenade got him and anyone coming up directly behind him. Later, as we moved out, we checked, and there were two dead NVA behind the bank, that was number 7 and 8 confirmed for me. A confirmed kill was one that could be authenticated by another Marine. We also kept track of estimated kills, those that could not be confirmed because of battlefield conditions. My unconfirmed kills were at this time at one hundred three. At first, I was annoyed by this idea of keeping track of how many people I killed, but our officers insisted on this so that they could report effectiveness, not only for each battle but overall, for the unit.

We saw additional movement then in the jungle around us. I moved to the backup position since I had fired my rifle and they knew where I was. Within a few seconds of the relocation, an enemy chi-com grenade landed right in the hole where we were and went off. So, it was a good thing we moved. These enemy grenades were cone-shaped on the handle, just like ice cream cones. They would activate the grenade by twisting the handle. In dense jungle like this, they would often put them on the ends of bamboo sticks and fling them out for pretty good distances and with surprising accuracy. I suspected this one came from ahead, deeper in the jungle. I had my men fix bayonets as now it looked like a strong possibility of some hand-to-hand combat if they rushed us. We all started tossing grenades wherever we saw movement in the brush. Even though it was a dense jungle, I positioned my men so they could support each other. This meant that we were pretty close to each other but still far enough to not have an explosion take out more than a couple of us at a time. I did not want anyone to get lost out there as it would mean pretty much certain death.

Sergeant Hobbes came up from behind us and jumped into our position. This new fighting position was not as good as the last, just a slight depression in the ground with a felled tree in front of it, but what was good about it is we could look out underneath the tree, and the tree protected the tops of our heads. Hobbes said, "Hagedorn, what is going on?" I liked Hobbes a lot. We played chess together often. He was very good, but I always won. I had held the title for the Marine Corps champion chess player back in Hawaii, winning that title from Schweitzer on one rainy Sunday afternoon as we sat in the barracks. I had convinced Schweitzer to play with no time limit. I knew that if I had plenty of time to take my moves, I could win. We talked about playing together for several weeks, but I would not do it until the no time limit condition was met. One rainy Sunday when there was nothing else to do, we played. We started at ten in the morning and played until 6:00 p.m. Poor Schweitzer. I drove him crazy that day, took as much as thirty minutes to make just one move. He was pacing around the barracks, swearing and saying, "You're taking too long." I would just remind him of our deal. We did this over and over again. He was very frustrated and mad. He kept saying he should never have agreed to this stupid way to play chess. To him the championship was very, very important. This was part of my strategy. I knew he was much better than me, but I needed to throw him off. I need to get him mad, so he was not thinking straight. I needed to make him take an impulsive move without thinking. He did just that. After I took nearly an hour to make just one move, he just walked up to the board and without looking moved his queen. I then took her. I knew then that I was going to be the new champion. After a few more hours, I finally had him in check mate. Schweitzer was the recognized champ in the corps up until then, and now I am. Men would fly in from California, Okinawa, and from all over the country and world just to play him and try to get the championship. I basked in the notoriety. Then, early one Sunday morning, two Marines showed up at end of my bunk, asking if I was Lance Corporal Hagedorn, and one of them wanted to challenge me. They had flown all night on a transport from Guam and were there to grab off the championship.

Schweitzer never stopped complaining that I had cheated him. I just reminded him that I won according to our rules, but I did feel guilty. Schweitzer had become my friend in Hawaii. He was very smart but the worst person at military discipline. I guess I felt a little sorry for him because he had no friends. Everyone else at least tried to fall out for inspection with starched utilities and spit shined boots, but not him. He would show up for inspection with a wrinkled uniform fresh from the dryer with no pressing. His boots never saw polish, and his brass belt buckle also had never seen copper cleaner. He was what we called a "shitbird." The whole platoon would show up looking sharp but not him. There was some talk about giving him a "shower party" to try to get him to square away. I did not like this because it involved grabbing a guy from his bunk in the middle of the night, covering his head with a pillow so he could not identify who was doing it, tying his hands behind his back, then taking him into the shower and hitting him with soap bars rolled up in towels. This was usually done until the person was left in pretty bad shape so that they would "get the message" to straighten up. I saw the results of one, and it did not work. The guy only got worse. I think this was done in team spirit to get everyone to work together but often got carried away, seriously injuring the recipient. I told everyone not to do it. I had decided to take Schweitzer under my wing. I was going to work with him and show him how to be a "good" Marine. Of course, he knew immediately what I was trying to do and told me flatly, "Hagedorn, it won't work." Nonetheless, I tried. Back in those days, I thought everything was possible. I explained to him how to have one good uniform set aside. Get it starched and just keep it in the locker, then when a snap inspection comes along, change into it. Also, I told him, "You need to have one set of boots perfectly spit shined and put these on only for the inspections, along with a belt buckle that has been wrapped in cellophane, have that all ready, then just put it on, and you are ready." I picked out one of his uniforms and walked him over to the base cleaners. I told them "Heavy starch." Rather than polish his boots, he went and bought a pair that had been "pre-prepared." The belt buckle he did himself. The next day, we picked up his utilities, and they were perfect. Saturday, we had our next inspection, and we all looked great, especially Schweitzer. The men were all surprised, and the NCOs were delighted. Even the lieutenant showed signs of approval. The men, on the side, congratulated me for a job well done. I was proud of my accomplishment, and I had a new best friend, but it did not last. The next inspection, he was back to his old ways. I asked him to do it again, and he flatly said no. He said that it was not him, and he was not going to do it for this "chicken shit outfit." I did not like that. Well, that was Schweitzer and now, he was still my friend. Everyone else was so serious about the Marine Corps, but there was something about his rebel nature that I liked. We started going out on weekends to challenge Hotel Street, and we both did a good job of that. The others also began to accept Schweitzer as he was and thought of him as just a "colorful guy." I will never forget just before leaving for Vietnam, I was on mess duty. I had a big stack of dishes in front of me and I was slowly loading them into the large mess hall dishwasher. I was just thinking how it was hard to believe that in five days I would be leaving for Vietnam. Schweitzer suddenly appeared at the door. I had not seen him since we left Hawaii and went to Camp Pendleton to deploy to Vietnam. I was glad to see an old friend, especially before leaving for Vietnam. He did not say a word to me, just walked up to the huge stack of dishes in front of me and pushed them over sending the whole stack crashing to the floor. It made a loud crash as it hit. I glanced out at the staff master sergeant sitting with a group of other sergeants sipping coffee at one of the long tables. He was just about to take a sip when all of the plates hit the floor. He was sitting a little hunched over, and when they hit, he sat up straight and stopped the cup just as it was about to reach his lips. After a brief pause of less than a second, he finished his sip and hunched back to his conversation again. I looked at Schwietzer in disbelief and said, "Why did you do that?" Without a word, Schwietzer reached over and pushed a second set of dishes to the ground. I glanced again at the mess sergeant, who once again jumped but a little more this time. I expected him to get up out of his chair and come in at that point, but he did not. I was really surprised to see that Schwietzer seemed to know that he would not come in either. He then said simply, "I'm getting you out of here. We are going to go on vacation for a couple days before we go to Vietnam." I said, "What? We can't do that. We do not even have a pass or anything. We will be absent without leave (AWOL) and could go to the brig for that." He said, "We won't go to the brig. They will be sending us to Vietnam, and they want us there. When we get back, we will just stand Captain's Mast get a slap on the hand and be sent to Vietnam." I said, "But I have a perfect record. I do not want that on my record." He said, "Exactly! You are too perfect. No one likes a perfect Marine. You need a few hits on your record so you look normal." In a strange way, he made sense. As I took off my mess apron and followed him out the door, I asked, "Where are we going?" He answered "Tijuana, where else?" It sounded good to me, but I was worried about what would happen when we got back. We spent four days there until we were out of money, and we had a wild time. I did stand Captain's Mast, lost a month's pay, restricted for a month, and was told the only reason I did not get busted to private and thirty days in the brig was because they needed lance Corporals in Vietnam. The next day, I left for Vietnam. Schwietzer was completely correct about everything, right down to my court martial. I was glad we went, and it was the last time I saw Schwietzer and thanks to him, now I had the glitch on my record. I was a "real Marine" and a "real man" after my experiences in Mexico. As he put it, "Well, if you die in Nam, at least you won't be a fucking cherry."

My Good Friend Hobbes

Hobbes was our platoon sergeant, second in command to Lieutenant Hawkins. This was the first time I had seen him since last night when we were in the bunker playing chess. He loved the game. He was one of the best I had ever played. He reminded me of one of those Marines in the World War II movies. He really looked the part. He always had the stub of a cigar sticking from the corner of his mouth. He looked very rugged and even a little mean, but once you talked with him, you found that he was one of the nicest guys. Hobbes was on his second tour in Vietnam. At first, I was astounded to hear this. I did not think anyone could make it through two tours in Vietnam. Then I asked him what he did on his first tour. He said, "It was easy; I just drove a truck around Da Nang." He was with transportation on the first tour and did not really see too much action. Hobbes had a wife and two young children. He showed me a picture of them one night as we sat and drank some scotch that my brother sent me. At first when I tried the scotch, I thought it was bad, never really had had scotch before. He grabbed it from me and tried it, pronouncing it "great, one of the best," and then proceeded to finish it off. Hobbes was a little crazy, I thought, or very brave. He would stand during ambushes and artillery attacks, not bothering to take cover. He now just had moved to the top back edge of our little fighting position and sat there, casually surveying the jungle in front of him. I told him he should get down; they were all over in front of us, but he just gave me a little quick smile and a wink. I continued to explain the situation to Hobbes and told him that they were moving around in front of us, trying to make him aware of the danger. I did not want him to use his rifle, so I gave him a grenade. I told him, "Don't use your rifle if you see something. Use the grenade so they do not know where we are at." Again, he just gave a little smile but took the grenade. I decided that I may as well show some bravery and moved up next to him on his left side. The other Marine in the hole looked at us like we were both crazy and I suppose we were. Then it suddenly happened. The explosion was very close, right next to Hobbes on the right side. We did not hear it coming in. When they are right on top of you, there is really no time, and you cannot hear them. When they are a little further away, you can hear the whistle as they approach. Also, I think this one was a mortar. They are very quiet coming in and especially when they land close. I did have time to crunch my neck down and turn my helmet to the side, toward the explosion. I heard the ping of shrapnel hitting my helmet and felt the jerk of my M16 as shrapnel hit that. My body was completely protected by the body of Hobbes. I was looking down and saw him slowly open his hand and the grenade rolled out. There was blood on it. Then I saw blood on his hand. I felt something wet and warm on my face, like the warm rains that fell there so often. I looked up. Hobbes was spouting blood from a bad wound in his neck. I reached up to compress the wound, but before I could get there, a big chunk of metal dropped from the artery and blood began to gush out. I looked into his eyes, knowing this was his last few seconds. He was looking at me. He tried to say something. I watched his lips move, but no words came out, and then he died. I felt his spirit leave the body. It seemed I could see it lift off as a misty shadow. I knew his body was just material now, and I could feel the emptiness of it. As always, it gave me a very lonely feeling. I said the Lord's Prayer. I was sad, but I was glad I was there when he died. I thought that it must be very lonely to die all alone. Some men dying alone, at night, when we could not get to them, sounded so scare and lost, often calling for their mothers and God until the very last moments. It was very sad. When I was younger and more foolish, I thought that I was so good I could keep everyone alive by my skill and bravery, but soon I learned I could not. So, then I made a new promise to myself and God. The promise was that I would try to be with all my men and my friends as they died. I hope Hobbes was happy that I was there, but maybe it does not really matter when you are dying. I still wonder what he was trying to say.

I sent the Marine in the hole with me back to let the lieutenant know what had happened. He came back about fifteen minutes later with three other Marines. The one in the lead looked a little shocked. They did not say anything. They just picked up his body and left.

I was very sad. Then I did something strange. I set my rifle down and went to the bottom of the hole. I curled up in a little ball and laid there. I do not know what the matter with me was. I just did not want to do it anymore. I wanted to die and get it over with. I prayed to God to just let me die, now. Then I saw the angel. She was in a mist, and it looked like there were more angels behind her. She had long blond hair and a pretty face with a slight smile. The smile was an interesting smile. It was as if she knew something. Then she spoke. She said, "Do you really want to die?" I said, "Yes" immediately. She said, "Are you sure? There are a lot of beautiful things in life that you will miss." I said I was sure, and that I could not take this any longer. Again, she asked if, I was sure. I told her again, yes. She said she would come back a little later and told me to think about it, and if then I still wanted to die, she would take me. I laid there in the hole and thought. I glanced at the other Marine and saw the deep concern in his face. I went back to my thoughts. I knew this was the moment to decide. In a bit, the angel did come back, and it looked like there were two other angels with her, standing just behind her. She said right away, "What have you decided?" I hesitated for a second and told her I wanted to live. She smiled a little more broadly and said, "I knew you would." They all just disappeared then. I did not tell anyone about this. I knew they would think I was totally crazy. I was not though. I knew this had happened and still know it. I have often thought that perhaps these were the spirits of the three little angels I was to father later in my life.

Horst Faas, Associated Press

Chapter 3

Another Time

March 6, 13:37:01

I sat up in the hole. Then picked up my weapon and got to the top next to the other Marine. I could tell he was relieved. He did not say a word. I am sure he thought I had gone crazy and was glad I was back. A lot of men did go crazy. It took several forms. Sometimes they became completely nonfunctional, just walking in a daze. The men were removed from combat on the next available helicopter. Other times they became very aggressive, especially toward the enemy. Some men that were slightly timid on the battlefield would become raging tigers, not able to wait until the next contact. These were kept in combat. I checked over myself for wounds. The only evident damage was my rifle. It had a hole completely through the stock where the shrapnel had passed, otherwise no other damage. Hobbes had been positioned to take all of the shrapnel except for the top of my helmet and my rifle. I had such mixed feelings and felt guilty that Hobbes had taken the full force of the explosion.

I told the Marine in the hole that I was going to check the men and see if I could find water and ammo for us and crawled out of the fox hole. I checked on the machine guns and told them to hold fire unless absolutely necessary. They all asked about Hobbes, and I could not say much. I decided to head back to the chopper area and see if I could locate extra ammo and grenades, especially smoke grenades and maybe some water. I made it down to where the landing zone (LZ) was established for the helicopters to pick up our wounded. I needed to rest and sit in some brush with other Marines guarding the LZ. The XO for the battalion (I had heard he was there each day through the previous assaults) came up to area where we were and indicated he would need a few men for a detail. I wondered, *what kind of detail? Maybe it was a good one. I knew some were. Most were not.* He knew where the last unaccounted for dead Marine was. He needed volunteers to bring him in. I wondered again, *what could be so bad about that but knew there were a lot of bad things out here?* I really did not want to volunteer for this one. I suspected it was not going to be good. Then I thought, *maybe this is the last thing then we go "home" for the night instead of staying out here.* I wanted to go home and not be out in the open overnight. I wanted to go back where there was plenty of food and water and more ammo. I was hungry and still thirsty but not as thirsty as before. It seemed to be a little cooler now. Even a degree or two lower made a big difference. He said, "Is there any NCOs in this group?" I hesitated to hope one would raise his hand before I did. None did so I raised mine. He glanced at me and said, "Good, you're in charge." I wondered, *In charge of what?* He said, "All of you grab your gear and follow me." We pushed our way through heavy brush, up and down a dry ravine, and came to a clearing at the base of a hill. We took no fire. I was happy about that. In the brush at the edge of the clearing, the XO pointed across the clearing to the base of the hill and said, "There he is. You've got to get him. I do not care how you do it, but bring him in. This is the last unaccounted for Marine so that part of our job will be done," I asked if there was enemy up on that part of the hill. He said, "Yes, a lot." I thought for a few seconds about how to do this. It was not going to be easy. That dead Marine was their "bait," and we were the fish. They did not want us to take the bait. They wanted to catch fish. I thought maybe we could go around the edge (but there was steep cliff on either side of the clearing so no room to flank) and slowly move up, but I knew they would see us, and then a firefight would ensue, and we would have more wounded and dead to get back and probably not even get close to the dead Marine. I thought about smoke, but it was too far, about one hundred meters and plus that would tip them off that we were coming. I wanted as many surprises as possible. I made my decision. I called to the men around and asked for five volunteers. I did not know any of these men, and they did not know me, so I was surprised when hands shot up. I selected five, strong but lean (as we all pretty much were). I said, "Here is what we are going to do. I want all your gear off and do not bring your rifles. We are not going to be firing. We are going to be running, so if you are not fast, tell me now. I want just helmet and flak jacket." I said, "We are simply going to run as fast as we can across the clearing and grab the Marine and then run back as fast as possible. I want this to be quick and done before the enemy has a chance to zero in on us." The XO looked at me with a surprised expression; this was a very abnormal tactic; one the Marine Corps never uses. For one thing, we never leave our rifles behind, never. I expected him to say no but he nodded and said, "It's your operation." I knew this was very unusual and thought the XO may not agree, but I wanted something unexpected, fast, and organized, something the enemy would not be ready for. They also knew their enemy and were counting on us to go about this in a standard Marine Corps procedure, move, cover, fire, and move, a tactic I knew would leave all of us dead and fresh "bait." I needed something different here, and I thought this would for sure work, if we moved fast and did not hesitate.

I told the ten or so Marines that would cover us that they needed to start firing on fully automatic once they saw any flashes from the hillside but not fire until the enemy fired. They all nodded to me. I knew my group would probably take the first hit while we waited for the enemy to open up, but I needed as much surprise as possible. This is why I told my group to keep running even if they got hit. My plan was (this I did not tell anyone) I expected at least one of us to get hit. The reason I picked five others was so I could help anyone wounded, while the other four carried the dead Marine. Four was enough to carry him and still run fast, but if we did not get hit, six would work even better. I had thought about eight going out, but that was more than really needed, and if this went wrong, there would not be as many dead. Also, eight of us running would attract more attention faster than six of us. I checked the five. One had forgotten his cartage belt was on with a canteen. I asked him to take that off too and briefly wondered if he had water in it. We were ready.

David Hume Kennerly, Getty Images

Chapter 4

Run like Hell

We ran like hell. I yelled, "Don't stop even if you get hit. Keep going." About halfway across the clearing, they started firing. The Marines behind us opened up fully automatic. A few bullets hit the dirt around us as we ran full tilt, to our objective. We were totally committed to this point. We got to the dead Marine, and I grabbed his right arm. I looked at his face. It was white and pale. He had glasses on, but the lenses were all shattered. I saw his double chevrons on his lapel. He was a Corporal just like me. I could not see any obvious wounds and wondered where he was hit. As I tugged on his arm to carry him, it came completely off his body. I did not hesitate but immediately grabbed his shirt. We all grabbed hold and started running. We were just about to when they first started firing at us. I was looking down at the ground, watching the man's legs in front of me. The fire was intense; rounds were hitting everywhere around us. Our Marines in the brush were firing as much as they could, but the enemy ignored them. They wanted us. I saw it hit his leg, the back of his leg behind the knee cap. It blew through and out the front. I saw the blood and pieces of bone spatter out onto the dry ground. The black Marine screamed and yelled, "I'm hit. I'm hit." I yelled, "You got to keep going. We can't stop now!" He did. He knew he had to or die. He slowed a little as his full run turned into a hobbled run, and he was dragging his left leg a little, but he kept going. I was surprised to see a man with such a serious wound continue to run. I was glad because I wanted to get all of us to safety as fast as possible. The bullets continued to pound around us as we kept running. We were now less than ten meters away from the relative safety of the brush when it happened. The lead Marine on the far side stepped on a land mine. At the time I did not know what it was, what had happened, and it was not until twenty years later that I remembered the details and finally knew what had happened and that it was a land mine, not a mortar or artillery. I think I had trouble with this because the XO did not tell me there was a mine field there. I think he kept the information to himself because he needed that last Marine back. I do not know what I could have done differently and still be successful though, and I was successful. We got the dead Marine, but the price was high, and we did not leave the enemy with the opportunity of fresh bait. But we did add five more dead Marines to the cost of the combat that day. All six of us, or should I say seven of us, went flying, mostly in pieces. I was blown straight up into the air. At first, I did not know it had happened. Then I realized my feet were not touching the ground. I was flying up and up, my feet still moving in a comical motion like a cartoon character. After I became aware of this, I had to make myself stop moving my feet. I continued up a little further and then started to fall back to earth. I think I went up about forty feet total. When I hit it, it was solid on my back. That knocked all the wind out of me. I could not move. At that point I realized we had been hit but thought it was a mortar. For years I thought that, but then in a dream, the memories came back. I had a continuing dream for many years that I was in a cartoon, and I was falling, and my legs kept moving like I was running. I thought this was funny and looked stupid, and in my dream, I would make my legs stop. I was told by girlfriends in later life that I was asleep; moving my feet back and forth like I was running. Often, they would shake me awake. I would be all sweaty, and they would ask what was wrong? I would tell them I had a dream about a cartoon, and they would say, "That shouldn't make you all sweaty." I thought so too. Then finally, so many years later, in a dream, I found out what this was all about. I finally was able to dream the whole dream, woke up, and understood.

Luckily, we were close enough to the line that some Marines were able to crawl out to us and drag us back in. I tried to move after I hit the ground but could not. I felt like I was paralyzed and wondered if I was hit in the spine. My head worked ok, but I could not get my body to function, not even a hand. I remember asking the Marine as he pulled me back to safety, "What happened?" He told me, "It was a mine." I also asked him how the others were, and he said, "Not good." I remember I was so happy he came to get me, and he did not even know me. The fire was intense with bullets landing all around us, but he continued to drag me. When he got me back to safety, a corpsman came over and looked at me. He checked me over then gently rolled me over to look for wounds on the back side and then rolled me back. He said, "Not wounded. You, OK?" I asked, "How come I can't move?" He said, "Just lay there for a while, and all the feeling will come back. In explosions, this happens to most people. They can't move for a while afterward." I then said, "What about the others?" He said, "No one made it. You are lucky. I will check on you a little later." He left, and I laid there for about ten minutes, watching the activity around me, wondering if I was going to get back to normal. After another five minutes, I could move my hands and arms, then my legs a little, then my toes. Feeling was coming back to my whole body. I was relieved. After a little longer, I sat up then got to my feet and went looking for my equipment that I had left behind earlier, along with my helmet, which was blown off. I got my rifle, pack, and cartridge belt then saw my helmet, out in the field. I really liked that helmet and had since I enter Vietnam. Funny the things we get attached to. That helmet was my pillow at night and my sanctuary during the heat of the day. We had been through a lot together, but I was not going out there for it. I decided to take one left from one of my dead Marines. As I took it, I felt as though the Marine was watching me and was honored that I wore his helmet. I felt honored to him. There was no bigger honor than to do what he had just done. To give his life to others was the very biggest sacrifice. To continue living is just what we all tried to do. His helmet fit perfectly.

The Marines never left a dead or wounded man behind. This has been tradition in the corps since the beginning. Many other Marines had died just like my Marines that day. This is the way it was, even though it did not seem to make sense sometimes.

The APC Incident

This had happened to me one time before in Vietnam when I was in another explosion that left me totally unable to move. It was a very strange situation and one that I thought for sure would kill me. This was back in August of 1967, and I had only been in Vietnam a couple months. It all started over the rifle I was issued.

When I first got to Vietnam, Hall (then private first class) and I (a Lance Corporal) were being issued our new M16 rifles. We had had no training with these weapons, and we were going into combat with them. We did not even know how to take them apart to clean them. We trained extensively with the old M14 rifle, and I was qualified as an expert with that rifle. Marksman with the 45 pistols and expert with the M60 machine gun, but I had never even held the "new" M16 rifle. It was drastically different from the M14. It was all pretty much plastic and so light weight I wondered how it could fire bullets that could kill. It looked and felt like a toy gun. We were taken out of the trash dump at Da Nang by a Corporal and given a quick fifteen-minute crash course in the firing and maintenance of the weapon. The Corporal giving the class mostly concentrated on making sure the sights were adjusted so that the weapon hit relatively close to the tin cans we aimed at. He then warned us that they jammed easy, especially on automatic, but we did not have to worry about automatic because these were not set for automatic. He said that any sand or dirt in them would freeze them up so we must keep them really clean. He said that the problem was that the expended cartridge would not extract from the chamber. With that stuck in there, you could not get the next bullet into fire. He warned that we had to keep the magazines really clean and the bullets clean, or we would jam. The extractor would not grip and pull out the expended cartridge and often not even when everything was really clean. I asked why we were using them if they did not work well. He said, "We just follow orders (I heard that a lot), and these are the weapons they have chosen. Besides they are working on the problems and new ones will be coming out soon."

In a rifle fire team, we were instructed usually only one person had the automatic set up on their M16, and this was to conserve our supply of bullets. Once in the field, I learned that everyone's weapon was modified to be automatic, so much for the instruction matching up to the real world. It was a quick adjustment to the trigger mechanism. After the Corporal was satisfied with our "sighting in" of the weapons, he pulled me aside and told me that he had given me one of the newer weapons. He said there were not very many of them out yet, but he had managed to get a few. He said that this was a good one and would not jam on me. This could mean the difference between life and death. I do not know why he was so nice to me. I guess he liked me. He was right about my weapon. I modified it for fully automatic, and it never jammed on me even in heavy combat when it got pretty dirty, and I had to fire it constantly. I was very thankful to him. I knew that he had probably just saved my life. If I ever meet him again, I will let him know he did just that. Later, in battle, I was to find many men dead with jammed rifles lying next to them. He was right; they did jam easily. They cost a lot of Marines their lives. It was many months later that the new M16 finally came to our unit, and everyone got one. Before that, can you imagine coming up against an enemy with automatic AK47, large-caliber weapons, and having only a small-caliber weapon and being able to fire only one time before it jammed? It was the worst nightmare and one of the reasons we started carrying so many grenades. Grenades and fix bayonets were the order of the day until the new rifles arrived.

When I joined Charlie Company in Quang Tri in June 1967, I was of just a few that had a good weapon. In early August, four of the infantry riflemen from second platoon noticed that I had a good one and asked me if they could have it. A pretty crazy request I thought. Why would I give up one of the best weapons in the company? I said, "No, this is the weapon I was issued." They said, "But you do not walk point and get into heavy firefights like we do, and we need the reliability of your weapon." I said, "I need to support my machine guns and protect my squad with firepower. I do need to have a reliable weapon, and I do engage in the same kind of firefights you are in. I have been ambushed five times since I arrived, and so I need the firepower too." They were not happy and cursed. They turned and walked away but threatened, "We're going to get that rifle." And they did try again. They returned a short time later with their lieutenant who ordered me to give them the weapon. I said to the lieutenant, "Sir, I must respectfully decline, Sir." He got very mad and yelled, "Are you refusing a direct order?" I said, "Sir, I was instructed to hang on to this weapon, and you will have to talk to my Lieutenant Hawkins. If he orders me, I will yield the weapon, Sir." I knew that minimally Hawkins would reissue it to one of the riflemen in our platoon, and we would still have it with us as firepower. Soon both lieutenants walked over. I had never talked to two lieutenants at once before, and I was very nervous especially because of the subject of the discussion. Hawkins said, "Lance Corporal, I want you to keep that weapon and use it in support of my platoon." I had direct orders that I liked very much. That really pissed off the other lieutenant, and he turned and stormed away.

I thought that was the end of it but not nearly; there was a lot to come as the result of this. A few days later, while Hawkins had gone to Da Nang to take care of some business, the second platoon lieutenant walked up again and said, "We are all going to the river to clean up." I immediately reached for my weapon. The lieutenant said, "The area is secured, so leave your rifles behind." Marines never leave their rifles behind. In boot camp, they made us sleep with our rifles on our chest, to drive home the point that a Marine and his rifle are never separated, and that they are the most important thing we have. I already knew what he was planning. When I got back, I knew there would be a different rifle there, and it would not be a good one. I also knew what I would do. I would immediately go to Hawkins and inform him what the lieutenant had done. I knew I would get my weapon back, and this guy would not get away with it. Lieutenant Hawkins was a very good lieutenant, and I trusted him completely. I will tell you a little bit about Hawkins in a moment.

We had to walk to the river, which was about three miles away. I felt very uncomfortable without a rifle. I did manage to borrow a 45 pistol and had that on my hip, but none of the other men had any weapons, leaving us very exposed if something did happen. We got to the river, and most of the men jumped in, but I did not. I was too concerned about an ambush and knew that this area was not all that safe as the lieutenant had indicated. I certainly did not want to be caught with my clothes off, in the river, if we were attacked. I was concerned that the enemy was watching, as I knew they always were, and could see that we were completely unarmed. I was very concerned that the lieutenant had us go to the river without weapons. I thought that if there was a sizable force around, and there probably was, they would take this opportunity to attack us. We were at the river for about an hour and then started to walk back to the perimeter. I could see a line of APC coming down the road moving toward our perimeter. These vehicles looked something like tanks with treads on them, but they were not armed with weapons, and the armor plating was not nearly as solid is a tank. They had a plank that they lowered in the back to let the men in and out. The lead APC pulled to a stop next to me, and the driver popped his head out the top. "Hey, you want a ride?" he said. I said, "Sure, beats walking." He lowered the plank, and I and sixteen other Marines filed in. The APC had seats on either side so that we sat facing each other. I sat near the front, but the driver motioned me to come up and sit next to him. He asked, "Are you an officer?" because I had a pistol on my hip. I said, "No, a Lance Corporal, machine guns." He said, "Good, thought you were with the pistol." He then said, "I didn't see you guys with any rifles." I told him that "The lieutenant had us leave them behind because he thought this was a safe area." The driver glanced around and said, "Well, I don't know about that. It doesn't look so safe to me, and you're always supposed to have your rifle." I said, "You got one?" hoping he would say yes. He shook his head no and said, "Nope, just a pistol like you." Well, at least we have two pistols now. We drove on through a flat rice paddy area about a mile from the perimeter when it happened. *Ambush*!

I was looking out the side window and saw them pop up out of the ground less than ten meters away. They just threw up the mat covering their small hole, immediately stood, and fired in one smooth motion, no hesitation. They were so close, they could not miss, and they didn't. I saw the RPG round coming right at us as if in slow motion. It went straight to the side of our vehicle and right in the middle of the APC. I felt it slam into us. I turned my head to look in the back and actually saw it tear though the metal on the side, throwing the Marines sitting there out of the way. It moved as if in slow motion to the inside center of the vehicle and then, as if something alive, evil, and sinister; it seemed to hang there for a second and inspect us as if we were food. I put my head down, looking at the deck, knowing what was next. The explosion was tremendous. There was instant carnage everywhere. Shrapnel bounced around the inside, against the metal, like ping pong balls. I knew it must have killed everyone in the back of the vehicle in that instant, and it did. I looked over at the driver. He was badly wounded, and I could tell immediately he was not going to make it. He had many holes in the right side of his chest, arm, and leg. The shrapnel had gone right though his flak jacket. A large piece of shrapnel about the size of a fifty-cent piece dropped from his neck right at the corduroyed artery. The stream of blood poured out, across the aisle between us, and covered my left side, some spattering in my face. I wondered if I was bleeding like that too but was pretty sure I was not hit. I was suffering from concussion. I could not move any part of my body but my head. I glanced at my legs and chest to make sure. I then stared at the driver, wishing I could do something for him. I knew that we were the only two left alive at that point in the vehicle, and I did not want to lose him too. He looked at me and said, "I am dying, aren't I?" I said, "Yes." Then he really surprised me. He gave me a slight smile. He said, "Let's go get them." I was surprised that he could even move, especially given how badly he was injured and surprised he wanted to get them. I thought quick and said, "OK." I said OK for a couple reasons. First, I knew everyone was unarmed in the other APCs. I also knew that standard procedures were for the APC to "circle up" sort of like in the old western movies where they would have the covered wagons get into a circle so they could fight the Indians. I knew that if this ambush was a big one, and there were a lot of enemies, they would wipe us out before help (men with rifles) could arrive. I thought this was a big ambush because there were a lot of us, and just a few NVR would not take that many of us on without strength even if they knew we had no rifles (and I think they knew). The enemy knew exactly what we would "normally" do in this situation, and I think they were going to take advantage of our weakness. I am sure the plan here was to wipe us out to a man, and I thought it would succeed because we had no weapons to fight back with. I knew we had to do something different here for any of us to survive. APCs never went across rice paddies and only stuck to the main roads in Vietnam. Yep! This would be unusual and might just do the trick. The trick was simple. Just do something, anything the enemy did not expect to throw them off and give us a chance. The driver asked, "Are you sure?" That was nice of him. He knew he was going to die, and he was worried about me. He knew I was not wounded and might otherwise have a chance at living. He knew I was pretty much defenseless and would probably wind up dead too, but I said, "Yes, let's go get them!" I had thought about it. I don't think I had a choice anyway, either to die now or in another half hour as they overran us all. I am pretty sure the driver was thinking the same thing and decided that at least we might be able to save the others.

And We Went to Get Them

He turned the vehicle on a dime, aimed it directly at the hole where the enemy had fired from, and ran right over them. I could see the hole was not deep when they stood and fired at us, probably because they did not have a lot of time to prepare for us when they set up this ambush. We ran over them and killed them and continued across the rice paddy. Explosions from mortars were going off all around us. Bullets were bouncing off the front of the vehicle as we approached the line of jungle that held the main force. I saw a couple of the enemy in the jungle line stand and fire at us with their rifles. Machine gunfire rattled across the front of us; it did not penetrate. A mortar round hit the top of the vehicle toward that back but did not penetrate either, I think. They were throwing everything they could at us. I could see a slight mound directly in front of us, and that is what the driver was aiming for. There was machine gunfire coming from it, and by the sound of the bangs on the APC, it was a heavy gun; luckily not heavy enough to penetrate the APC's steel hull. The vehicle went up the mound easily, with no effort, knocking over small trees and brush. We crested the mound, and the vehicle came down hard facing downward on the other side of the mound. The machine gun was squashed underneath us. The driver got it! At this point, the driver died. He had gone as far as he could, and he did a really good job. I was surprised he lasted as long as he did. I am sure there was no blood left in his body even before we reached the mound where the machine gun had been spewing out bullets, but he was able to complete his objective. He went up the mound and right over the machine gun coming to rest at a sharp angle facing down the other side of the mound of dirt.

I looked in front of me, not believing what I saw. There were over three hundred NVA in front of me, all regular army with all the gear. This was a very organized unit, a well-equipped unit. I could see about half the perimeter around me. They were dug in and looked like they were ready to stay and fight, but then I saw some on the far end gathering up their gear and starting to run in the opposite direction, back into the jungle on the far side. Then more stood up and picked up their gear. Soon, most were heading in the opposite direction. It looked like our plan worked. Many of the enemies that were closer to me were looking at me nervously and wide-eyed as they picked up their gear. I could see they were surprised I was there. I think the enemy officers at that point thought it was a full-scale attack by us, and that since we had already breached their perimeter, they decided to get out of there. This was normal for them. They would stay and fight if they thought they had the clear advantage over us; otherwise, they would cut and run. Perhaps they could not see the far side where I had come from, so they did not know that the unit was not attacking. I think they did not realize that just one solo APC had breached their line but thought rather that our whole unit was attacking and already inside their perimeter.

This was all happening very fast. I then saw four enemies directly in front less than two meters away slightly below my field of vision just staring at me with surprised looks on their faces. They were the team from the machine gun we had just run over. They must have backed out of the position just as we got to it. I mused for a second that they had four assigned to the machine gun just like us. I just looked at them, and they just looked at me. I was trying to reach for my 45 but could not make my arms work. I saw the one a little in back of the three, studied my face intently and saw a small smile come to his mouth. I knew he then realized I was disabled and probably wounded. He slowly reached into the pack of the man in front of him and pulled out a chi-com grenade. I watched him twist it to activate it. He then tossed it in through the top open hatch of the vehicle. It landed right next to me and between me and the driver. At that point, they just turned and moved away to join their main group. One of them glanced back at me as they moved away. I wondered if he felt sorry for me. He did not look as if he was happy; in fact, I thought I saw a look of concern on his face. Funny, this is war, and we are trying to kill each other, but there is still some room for humanity left in most of us. I tried to reach the grenade so I could throw it out but still could not get my body to function. My arms felt as if they were not there. I could not make my hands move. My body was completely numb except for my neck and head. I thought, well, this is it. This grenade is so close to me, there is no way I will survive this. I turned my head to the window but knew my whole body was exposed, and when this went off, it would pepper me with shrapnel. I prayed, and I waited for the explosion.

I thought I heard a faint noise and decided to take a last look at the grenade and perhaps try to reach it. Then incredibly I saw a black hand grab the grenade. There was a Marine with me. How could that be? I thought, *this is impossible!* He tossed it back up and out of the hatch. It was barely outside when it exploded, but we were protected by the armor of the vehicle. I was astounded to see the Marine standing there. I had come out of nowhere. Then I remembered the driver told me as we just started to climb the mound that he would lower the back ramp just in case anyone was alive and in case I needed to get out. I thought then and knew that no one could possibly be alive back there. The Marine standing next to me told me that when our APC attacked, he thought everyone was going to attack so he ran out behind the vehicle as we crossed the rice paddy. He had followed and was in the middle of the rice field before he realized he was the only one following us. I was glad to see him and glad he made it. I thought that if he thought everyone else was attacking, then the enemy might think so too. That is what I was hoping that the enemy thought too. I said, "You came after us without a rifle?" He said, "I thought I would be able to get one on the battlefield as things developed." He said he did not realize no one else was attacking until he was halfway out in the paddy and way too exposed to go back to the unit. At any rate, I was very glad to see him, at that point; I thought I might just have a chance of survival. It was very brave of him to come after us and especially without a weapon.

He took a long look at the enemy situation in front of us then the driver and said, "Looks like he is dead." I said, "Yes, he died just as we got to the top of the mound." He looked at me over and could see that I was not bleeding and said, "Well, let's get the hell out of here." I said, "I can't move." He asked if I was hit, and I said, "No, just concussion I think." He reached down and grabbed me by the shirt and put me across his back in a fireman's carry and started out the back of the vehicle. It was a real mess in the back. A lot of the Marines were totally unrecognizable. There was blood and body parts all over. The floor was covered thick with blood. The Marine slipped twice in the blood, and we nearly fell to the deck, but both times he managed to get his balance again. And then, suddenly, we were outside in the bright sun. I was glad to be outside. If I was going to die, I wanted to be outside. He started running with me on his back. Bullets started hitting the ground all around us. I thought, well I guess not the entire enemy had run off into the jungle, and judging from the number of bullets, a lot of them had remained to hold the position or perhaps had taken up a new position. As usual, in this kind of situation, they left a detachment behind to hold off the Marines while the primary unit escaped. So, they were the ones firing at us now. I was watching our shadows as he ran. I was wondering if I would get hit in the back at any second. I just watched our shadows on the ground and all the bullets sending up clouds of dust as they dug into the earth around us. I expected to feel a bullet hit me at any second. It seemed like a very long run, and I did not really think we were going to make it to the unit, but we did.

He carried me in among the circled APCs and gently laid me down. He asked, "Are you OK? Did you get hit when we were running?" I said, I thought I was OK but still could not move. He then asked if I was an officer; because of the pistol on my hip, and I guess because I was up front with the driver. He said he hoped I was an officer so he could get a medal. He wanted a medal. Just then, a corpsman came over followed by an officer. The corpsman carefully looked me over; turning me on my stomach to check for back wounds then rolled me on my back again and pronounced me fine. I did not feel fine. He said, "It will take a little while, but soon everything will be working just fine again." The officer then said, "Is there anyone else alive in there?" looking in the direction of the APC. I said, "No." He asked, "Were you driving that?" I said, "No, the driver was alive for a while, and he drove it into the enemy then died as we got to the top of the machine gun position. I was sitting next to him." He asked, "How many are in there?" I said, "About fifteen or sixteen." He shook his head and looked down. There were actually seventeen, counting the driver and me. He said, "I'm going to recommend both of you for medals." The Marine who had saved me was still around and interrupted "What about me, Sir? I ran out there and saved this guy," nodding his head in my direction. The officer glanced at him and said, "This guy and the driver saved the whole unit, over a hundred Marines, and equipment." There was no protest from the other Marines. I did think he deserved a medal for getting me but knew it was the officer's decision. I then said, "The medal should be for the driver. I was pretty much along for the ride, and it was his idea to attack." The officer thought for a second and said, "OK, but give me your name, Rank, and unit." I did. He walked away, and then the other Marine left, grumbling something as he went. He should have gotten his medal; he deserved it. I just laid there for a while watching the activity around me. After a while, the feeling started coming back in my legs and arms, and I could move my hands again. I sat up, then got up a little unsteadily but getting my balance. I walked back to the perimeter with a group of Marines who were heading back. I did not want to ride in one of the APCs that were available. I declined several offers. I never wanted to ride in one again. From then on, I just wanted to be in the open and not in any type of vehicle, no matter how far the walk. That applied to helicopters too now. When I had to get into one, I felt very uncomfortable. I went to my bunker. The first thing I looked for was my rifle. I had not forgotten about it in all the commotion. Yep, my rifle had been replaced by another just as I expected it would. Well, I would take this up soon with Hawkins who I had heard arrived back while we were out. I sat on the edge of my bunker in the hot sun, just sort of dazed by everything that had happened. I could not believe I had gone through all of that and survived. I looked my body over and felt pleasure at seeing my feet and legs attached, a very strange feeling. One of the Marines in my squad showed up a little later and said, "Wow, wasn't that something." Not really concentrating, I said, "What?" He said, "That ambush. I really thought they had us, but how about that one APC that broke it all up? I heard only one guy got out of it alive;

the lucky son of a bitch." I looked at him and said, "It was me." He said, "You're shitting me?" I said, "No, really. It was me." He said, "Fuck!" Later he told Lieutenant Hawkins. The officer with the ambush also talked with Hawkins about me. After a couple hours and still a little dazed, I did go off and find the lieutenant to let him know my rifle was missing and replaced it with another, one of the ones that did not fire well and that would jam when on automatic fire. He immediately wanted to know how I could go without my weapon. Good question, one I had anticipated. We were meticulously trained never to be without our weapon. I told him that it was a direct order from the second platoon lieutenant. He said, "Fuck" too and walked off in the direction of second platoon. I went back to my bunker. About fifteen minutes later, the same three guys (minus the fourth) from the second platoon showed up and handed me the weapon. It looked like mine. I saw the small hole in the stock of the weapon from the shrapnel made when Hobbs died, but I checked the serial number (which we were made to memorize) just to be sure. This one was mine. They actually said, to my surprise, they were sorry, but they really needed it. The other guy previously with them had died the day before with a jammed weapon. They said they were sorry, and that is why they took it. I said I understood, and that I was sorry to hear about their dead friend. They turned and walked away. I wished and prayed that we could all have good weapons. I did say a prayer then asking God to get us the weapons as soon as possible and to bless the dead Marine. The weapons did arrive a few weeks later. We still died but not from jammed weapons.

Lieutenant Hawkins asked me the next day if I got the weapon back. I told him, "Yes, Sir" and mentioned that they apologized and told him about their dead friend. He appeared to be relieved that there were some reasons they took it. He then said that he had heard about what had happened in the APC ambush, and that he wanted to recommend me for a medal. I thought for a second, a medal would be nice but really seemed somewhat unimportant. I thought briefly that it might not mean as much at that point; I did not think I was going to survive a whole lot longer. I explained to him that it was primarily the driver who deserved this not me, and that there was a black Marine that actually saved me who also deserved a medal. He said, "I don't care. You were a big part of it, and you should have the medal." I thought for a second and suggested an alternative that he liked. I said, "This is a lot of paperwork, correct?" He said, "Yes, but I have a lot of paperwork to do already." I said, "Instead of a medal for me, would you consider writing a letter to the family of any guys who die or are seriously wounded in our platoon to let them know what happened?" He thought for a second and said that he was already doing that, but he would spend a little more time with it. I heard from my secret spy, the radioman, that he did do this. I know my family would have liked to receive a letter from Hawkins if something happened to me, and they would rather have that than a medal. The medal issue, however, did not end here.

Several weeks later, I was resting on the sandbags of our deep bunker near the door, after we had completed a night ambush, ready to jump in if I heard the guns popping in the north. I saw a small chopper (not at all one of our normal supply choppers or standard medevac choppers) approaching the perimeter from the direction of Da Nang. I thought that was strange because it was not a medevac or a supply chopper. It looked more like a civilian helicopter but still painted green. I watched it slowly approach our perimeter and settle in softly on the landing pad. I was thinking that this would definitely attract the attention of the enemy forward observers (FOs), and we would soon be getting shelled by heavy artillery from the north. I watched as one Marine climbed clumsily out of the chopper. He was bright green. I do not think his uniform had ever seen the jungle before. Ours looked almost yellow from the color of the dirt but that helped us to blend in, sort of natural camouflage. He was definitely a target, and I was wondering if a sniper was aiming in on him right now, thinking he was a high-ranking officer—maybe he was. I watched as he made his way down the path from the landing zone (LZ). The radioman approached him to see what was going on, and then he pointed at me. The green overweight (at least by the standards of the lean Marines in the field) Marine began to make his way toward me. I thought this was strange. He was obviously from administration in Da Nang and had never been in the field before. Why did he want to talk to me? Did I do something wrong? When he got to me, I could see he was a buck sergeant. He wore his Rank on his collar. He said, "You are probably wondering why I am here?" I said, "Yes" as I glanced at his chopper, which turned the engine off completely. The pilot kept the propeller turning at a slow rate . . . I think the pilot knew what was going to be soon happening. The sergeant confirmed he was from Da Nang, and that he was here to talk to me about reenlisting for four years in the Marine Corps. I laughed. I said, "They flew you out here to talk to me?" He said, "Yes." I had never seen this happen before and thought it was very strange. He said, "If you reenlist, we will give you the Rank of sergeant and a month off anywhere in the world." I simply said, "No," and added, "Do you hear those booms in the north?" He said, "No." I said, "Listen carefully." He then said, "Yes, I hear them now." I said, "Those are the Vietnamese artillery guns firing, and soon thousand pounders will begin landing here." He stammered and said, "Why? How?" I said, "Your chopper attracted their attention, and this always happens when choppers land. You should get out of here as fast as you can. This area is soon going to be covered by thousand pounder explosions." He was administrator, but I think he knew what a thousand pounds could do. He immediately turned and started running for the chopper, that is, as best he could with his weight; it was more of a waddle run. The pilot saw him running back and immediately cranked up the propellers. I watched the chopper lift off as the first of the rounds screamed in. I went down back into the deep bunker, into safety. They began landing near where the chopper was, a total of about twenty rounds. If the chopper had been delayed much longer, it would not have made it. Funny they sent a man out to talk to me about reenlisting in the Marine Corps. I had not seen that before. I was actually giving it some thought but decided that if I re-upped, I was going to look for a better deal, maybe a promotion to officer. I thought I could make a good officer. I liked the sound of it First Lieutenant Hagedorn.

Associated Press

Chapter 5

Back up the Hill

March 6, 15:03:11

I returned to my squad, and a few asked where I had gone and why I had gone for so long. I told them briefly what had happened. They said I was lucky to have run through a mine field and made it alive. Yes, I was. About fifteen minutes later, the radioman appeared from the jungle behind us and said for us to "Get back to the platoon. We are going to continue the attack." We gathered our gear and moved back. It was well over a hundred degrees now. I was suddenly very thirsty, but my water was gone. Everyone was gone, and the heat would still be bad for several more hours. I wondered if I could make it without water. I said a prayer asking for help and protection. I found the lieutenant and requested orders. He said, "Corporal. Hagedorn, I am sorry about Hobbes." I said, "Thank you, Sir." He said, "I know he was a good friend, and I will write his family about him." He asked for some brief details on how he died. I could tell he was taking mental notes. He then told me to move up to the point squad and support them as best I could with the machine guns. He said, "We are going to take that hill now." I said, "Ay Hay, Sir" and moved my squad forward. I was excited about what I knew would happen next and prayed that we took only a few casualties.

I knew this would be difficult to do with the slope of the hill and brush in the way. Plus, you really need to have a defined position to deliver accurate fire with the guns, but I decided that for this final push we would need fire power and told the gunners they could now fire at will. They were very happy; they could finally open up the guns. This is what a machine gunner wanted to do the most, use the fire power of the M60 machine gun. I knew that this would be deadly, for both sides. My gunners wanted to do this ever since we began the attack up the hill, but I would not let them. They would be in the open and easy targets, and I knew the enemy would concentrate on taking them first. I still had both of them, and I thought this was a bit of a miracle. I wanted to keep both of them until this moment. I wanted to get them up the hill in good shape just for this assault. I knew if I used them earlier, they would not be here now. The guns were always targets; just a week earlier, I lost my best gunner and a good friend because he opened up in a situation that he shouldn't have. I was with my other gun when we encountered some sniper fire. I heard Vought firing the gun. As soon as I heard this, I left the fire team and went to where he was. By the time I got there, he was already hit. Shot right in the chest. I first said, "Damn it, you're not supposed to fire the gun for just a sniper." He said he was sorry, but the squad leader had ordered him to do it. I felt bad that I yelled at him and told him I was sorry. He was in pretty bad shape. I made sure his wound was compressed and got a corpsman to give him some morphine for the pain. I held him like I did all my men who were dying. When I was in training and after I first got to Nam, I made a promise to God that I would never lose a man. I soon found that I could not keep that promise because of all the combat and casualties, so I made a new one. The promise was that I would be with my men as they died, to at least offer comfort, no matter how bad the battlefield. That was a promise I could keep. Word got around through the battalion that I was doing this, and I was even asked to come hold other men that I did not know as they died. I became sort of a chaplain, I guess. I think that was because we did not have a chaplain out with us because of the danger. They certainly would not last long just as our corpsmen did not last long. The corpsmen were usually right in the middle of the fire, and the enemy would shoot them every time. We lost a lot of good, brave corpsmen, even though we did everything we could to protect them; they were trying to save us. As much as I could, I was with my men as they died no matter how bad the battlefield was. I would often get to one of my men and hold him, completely exposed to the rifle fire, but I would ignore that. My men and the others knew I would do this and would always fire to protect me as much as they could.

On March 6, I could not do this, as we had to keep the attack going, I could not stop for anyone, but I did say a prayer for them.

I do not know if Vought made it or not. I got him on a chopper, and he was still alive; I never heard anything regarding his condition. I knew it was serious enough that he would never be returning to combat, one way or another. Vought was a really good guy from West Virginia. He was tall, about six feet, three inches, handsome, and very soft spoken. I liked him the instant I met him. He wanted to be a gunner. He was missing his trigger finger on the right hand. I asked him, "What happened to your finger? I am not sure you can fire the gun." He said, "I can use my middle finger." He then explained that he lost the finger when a racehorse bit it off. He said, "In West Virginia, we have a lot of racehorses." That was a surprising story and interesting. I remember when he got to Nam he came up and asked me if he could be a machine gunner. I was a little suspicious; not many infantries wanted to be gunners, but I thought it might be good to have an infantry man combined with us. As I mentioned, the U.S. Marine Corps tactics for machine gun deployment with an infantry platoon was similar to what the Germans used in WWII. Funny that we modeled after them, an enemy we defeated. We also modeled after the Greek Spartans. This I had learned in boot camp. They told us that the Marine Corps was not afraid to take from the best military tactics in the world, including historical, and use it, incorporating these tactics to make themselves more effective as a fighting force. The Germans used the guns as the main focal point. Wherever the guns deployed for position and fields of fire, the infantry would then fill in around them in support of them. We liked to be on hills and across wide open areas. Of course, the way it really worked is that we all supported each other. It was all about the architecture of the battlefield, and that could be critical to both winning and staying alive. I was always careful to pick both good fields of fire combined with finding, as much as I could, good protection for the guns. The fallback position was also critical as it had to incorporate these features too. Many times, I watched a machine gun position enveloped by fire and explosions not only immediately after we left it, but as the battle progressed, the enemy seemed to think we were still there. When the fighting position got "hot," we would fall back to a secondary position we had preselected, which had a field of fire over the first position plus fields of fire that covered those of the original position (as much as possible). The enemy would avidly pursue that target, even though we were not there, and no fire was coming from there. It was like they had it stuck in their brains. I can understand it because in the heat of battle, you get an objective in mind and with all the confusion around, you just stick with that thought. Once I saw them looking all over a position after they reached it, thinking we must be still there, maybe just hiding? Funny! It seemed funny the first time I saw it. However, this was a real advantage because then they became targets as they concentrated on the wrong position, and we could easily take them down. Especially in darkness (when they usually attacked), confusion was the main ingredient, and this technique took advantage of the darkness and the confusion. I said to Vought, "Have you had the 0331 training for guns?" He said, "No, but I really want to be a machine gunner." That was pretty much good enough for me because not many wanted to be machine gunners. It was dangerous, and there was a lot of extra weight to carry with the gun and all the bullets. I told him this, and he said OK. I glanced at his size and knew the weight would not be a problem. But still I thought no one wanted to be a gunner unless they were crazy, and maybe we were. I said, "OK, I will train you." That was it; I trained him, and he went on to become the best in my squad and the second in charge. In training him, I tested him many times on the details of night fire, assaulting positions, fields of fire, cleaning and care of the guns and ammo, use of the tripod, and firing the weapon in a walking assault position. These were all things taught in school to the 0331-machine gunner. All the men looked up to him as a leader. He was a religious man and told me many stories about his family back home. He had a girlfriend that he planned to marry when he got back home. I was very sad and mad to lose him, especially when it was not necessary. I found the squad leader who ordered him to fire. I asked him, "Why the hell did you do that? You cost me my best man." He knew what I was talking about. He defensively said, "I needed the support." I said, "Don't ever do that again." He should have and did know better; I was very mad at him. Fact is, though sometimes, they did not know better. In combat, field promotions come overnight because of losses. A man may not be fully trained and ready to lead but must step into the position, like it or not, to take over a fire team, squad, or even a platoon. I supposed that this is what happened in this case; nonetheless, I was still mad. It was such a loss that did not need to happen. Rifle men take out snipers in the jungle, not machine gunners.

We made contact with the point squad. Our point squad was now the third squad, the reserve squad. That meant the first and second squads were pretty much gone. That left my full squad and nearly all of third squad to finish our attack. I looked around for Corporal Hall, the squad leader of the third squad but did not spot him. I found one of his men in a little open area sitting in a hole with his back to the enemy, just some brush covering him from enemy view. I wondered briefly why he did not get lower in the hole where there was more safety. That seemed a little strange, but strange things were happening everywhere that day. I made the mistake of thinking that it was safer than it really was because of the man position and seeming lack of concern. I squatted down next to him. I was squatting in the middle of a well-worn path that led up the hill to the north. I asked him if he knew where Hall was. He said he was off to the right flank checking his men. I was glad to hear he was still OK. I never did this but was so thirsty I asked if he had any spare water. He said, "Sure" and gave me a canteen that was nearly full. I wanted to drink the whole thing down but only took a couple swallows. I wondered how he could have so much water left as I moved the canteen toward my lips. As I held up the canteen and drank, I heard a bullet wiz by my helmet. It was very close. I have heard a lot of rounds come close, and this one was right next to my left ear. I fell to the ground completely and crawled into the hole. I didn't spill any water during this maneuver, which was good. I gave the man back his water and thanked him. He then said with sort of a slow drawl, "You shouldn't have sat there. Four Marines have been shot by a sniper in that same spot." I looked at him incredulously and asked, "Why didn't you say something right away." He shrugged his shoulders.

Then I could see he was not quiet all there mentally. His eyes were not focused, he had the stare, and he was actually in a different place. Then I understood but was not happy that I had come so close to dying. I was annoyed at myself for not being more careful and sitting in the open, on a path like that. *I should have known better and been more careful,* I said to myself. Generally, the enemy was not a good shot (unless they are sniper trained). If they were trained as well as we were, I would have been dead a long time ago. They were very good though with mortars and grenades. They must have practiced a lot to be so good with the bamboo poles and grenade placed on top then flinging them way out front. They seemed to always hit right next to or directly in our fighting holes. There was not much time left to try to grab them and throw them back because of the time used to get them on the pole and fling them out at us. Well, I was very glad he missed, and I guess he had had better luck earlier from what I heard from the crazy guy.

We all got the order to start moving up. I gathered up my men and warned them about the sniper ahead and told them to stay off the path because it was a killing field. My men spread out with guns online and the infantry of the third squad right with us. We had now become infantry. We did have the 50-caliber supporting us as we moved up, plus the mortars were landing shell after shell right on the ridge line, which helped a lot but the fire from the enemy still became very intense. We sure could have used some jets right now, but I knew they were not always available. There were a lot of explosions around us. I could not tell for sure if they were grenades or mortars or both. We again threw out smoke, which helped a little but this time they seemed to know right where we were at. Bullets screamed past my ears. They were hitting the ground around me and the men. Some were hitting the men. Branches and small trees were being cut down and falling on us as we moved. Dirt flew into the air around us and large clumps of dirt banged on my helmet. At this point, I could not hear a thing. My hearing was completely gone from all the loud explosions and rifle fire. This made it seemed surreal as we moved on up, little or no sound but all the activity going on. One thing was really good when this happened; it was less scary because there was not all the noise going on. If you could not hear the explosions, it did not seem as bad. Since the sound was missing, it almost seemed a lot like a bad dream, but not quite; I could still see what was happening. I saw a man fall on my right, not too far away and then another. I just kept moving and praying. I saw both my guns on either side of me firing but could not hear the fire. I prayed for all of us. I prayed very hard as we moved. An explosion went off in front of us but far enough away so that it did not stop us. The dirt just bounced off of us as we pushed forward. I could not hear it or see it but imagined the shrapnel zinging by our bodies. If anyone was hit by it, it did not stop us; we continued to move up. Sometimes, from light wounds because of the adrenaline going through your body, you do not feel it. I have seen many men hit, and they did not even know it. Some pretty seriously, but they were completely unaware of the wound. There was an incident, which I vividly remember where I and one of many Marines were in a shell hole, and another Marine came up to us somewhat casually as if nothing was going on. This was after a big artillery barrage from the north where they were firing thousand pounders at us. He did not have his weapon and did appear a little dazed but otherwise

OK, that is except for the fact that he was missing half of his head. A piece of shrapnel from one of the rounds had sliced neatly at an angle; across the left top part of his head, it looked almost surgical. The shrapnel must have been red hot, cauterizing as it went, because there was no blood. It obviously blew off his helmet, and there must have been enough shock that he was not really aware of what had happened. The wound went from right above his left, straight back at about a thirty-degree angle, taking off most of the top of his head. Most of his brain was gone, and he did not know it. The man next to me could not even speak because of what he was seeing. I said, "You got to get to a corpsman." He said, "Why?" I said, "You have been hit and don't know it." "Really, which way to the corpsmen station?" he asked somewhat matter-of-factly. I pointed, and he started off in that direction. It was one of the strangest things I ever saw, and I still can vividly picture it.

Korea Times

Chapter 6

Final Assault

March 6, 15:58:45

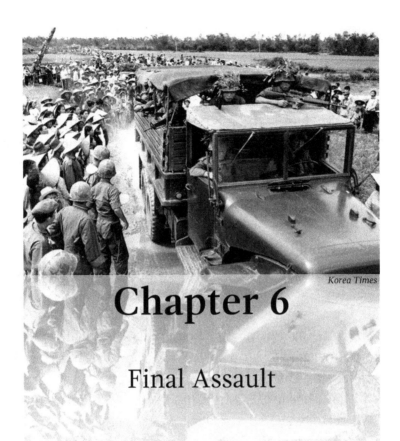

I figured we were now less than about fifty meters from the top; we were close, so close, but I knew this would be the most difficult part. We were passing by bunkers and trenches of pretty mammoth proportions, not like the individual bunker and occasional trench we were hitting earlier in the assault. They were all lined with sandbags and dug deep into the earth. The bunkers were well reinforced and looked like they could withstand one of our 105 hits but probably not one of our heavier artillery rounds and certainly not jets; oh, what I would give to see some jets stream overhead in support, but it looked like we would be doing this one on our own. There were a lot of dead enemies in the trenches, most shot but some hit by our grenades, mortars, and some by the 105s. The trenches were a mess, littered with debris, rifles, ammo, grenades, helmets, packs, and bloody bandages. They had put up a good fight here, but they lost, or at least were losing. I knew we could do this. There were body parts everywhere from the dead enemy. Although I had not heard our mortars or howitzer 105s firing during the attack (probably because of the loss of hearing), I could see the effect of their accuracy and skill all along the assault path, especially the mortars. I had new respect for the M60 mortars and the Marines who fired them. I was amazed that they could keep those heavy mortars moving up the hill behind us (especially in this heat) to be able to stop, place the mortars, fire, hit the enemy just in front of us (and not kill us, this was important, and difficult because it often had to be very close, ten or twenty feet away), then pick everything up and move forward to do it again, keeping pace with us as we moved. They had spotters with us whose primary purpose was to direct the fire in front of us. They were very good, better than I expected. As I looked around at their accuracy, I felt a little guilty that I thought only my machine gunners were the professionals and maybe the infantry guys we worked with, but pretty much that was it, well, of course, except for the Marine jet pilots and the Marine helicopter pilots and then again there was the navy supporting us. Well, I realized it was not just my guns. I know that those teams must have had the same regard, respect, and love for their weapons and jobs that we as gunners did for ours. It was very good to know that I was with experts. In a very strange way, I felt safe, even with all this death around me—very strange. Without the mortars, I do not think we could have made it, but then, every man is important in a place like this. As I was thinking about all of this, sort of daydreaming; I passed by one enemy who had his head neatly cut off at the top of his neck, blood still oozing from the open cavity. It was a fresh wound. I had passed several twitching, dying enemy on this assault. This particular enemy was in a sitting position against the back of the trench as if he had just sat down taking a rest. In his lap, his head sat looking forward, eyes wide open, as if it had been neatly placed there. I wondered if there was still some comprehension left in this man. I wondered if he could actually see me passing by. I think possibly. I think his brain was still active. If so, I wondered what his thoughts were. Did he have fear? Was he wondering what had suddenly happened to him as I did when I was blown in the air by the land mine? Did he want to try to get up to kill me? Yes, I think the last question was true. I had the feeling he saw me and wanted his body to work, to grab a rifle, and to kill me just like me trying to reach the grenade in the APC or reach my pistol to shoot the enemy who were about to throw the grenade. I thought, yes, he would try to fight to the end just like me and all the others out here that day, on both sides.

I thought that his head looked like we had placed it there. That maybe someone would do such a thing as a sort of joke, but I knew no one placed it there because we were the first up there. My mind strangely continued to wander for a second, and I thought that any Marines coming up behind us would think we did it. I pictured the smiles on their faces, them thinking that we had a strange sense of humor—all these strange thoughts. I got my mind back to concentrate on the work at hand. I wished we could stop and use these trenches as protection from the fire but knew if we did it would end the attack. We needed to keep the momentum going. We could not stop now. We had to just keep going no matter what, like it or not. My hearing was gone at this point, but I thought I could hear some dull explosions to the right flank where second platoon was making their assault and to the left flank where the third platoon was attacking. I thought that all three platoons were all almost online and all moving at the same pace to the top. This was perfect. Since we were the primary central attack force and because we had flanking platoons nearly extending around the hill, we could not be "flanked" by the enemy once we took the top. Also, any counterattack was then very unlikely as I was sure we were killing most of the enemy as we went. They would have none left to counterattack.

I could see a lot of enemies now. Some were standing outside their bunkers firing at us like before. We were firing as fast as we could; only taking long enough to eject a magazine when it was spent and shoving in a new one. From the corner of my eye, I saw one of my guns go down as the result of a big explosion. I quickly took aim at an enemy who was aiming in on one of the Marines near me. As I moved my rifle in his direction, another enemy popped up from a trench and took aim at me. I knew I could not get the guy who was about to get me and still shoot the one who was aiming at the other Marine; there would not be enough time to get both. I thought for a brief second about not shooting the one who was about to shoot the other Marine and just get the one threatening me. Then I decided I had to save the

Marine near me first, so I took aim and fire, hitting the enemy square in the chest. He went flying backward from the burst of M16 fire. I then moved my rifle as fast as I could back to the one who was going to shoot me. It seemed like everything was in slow motion, almost like a dream with things happening very slowly. I tried to move my rifle faster but could not go any faster than I was already going. I knew I was going to lose this one. There was just not enough time to get back to him. I was thinking that the bullet was already on the way and just waited to feel the impact. I did not give up though; he might have missed (not likely, we were too close) or have a jammed rifle, also not likely; the AK47 was a very reliable weapon and hardly ever jammed. As he came into my line of fire, I saw that he was crumpling to the ground. He had been shot by one of the other Marines with me. I was still alive! This was all happening very fast men falling on after the other on both sides. I took aim at another and fired, and another, and another, wondering when I would be shot. I was on fully automatic but fired burst of three rounds to conserve ammo. I need to conserve ammo (although it did not seem like the time to conserve ammo) because I did not know how much longer this would last, or if we took the top, if there might possible be a counterattack by the enemy.

I continued to move forward, firing and not bothering to take cover, not even crouching down, just moving, firing, and praying as I went. I prayed very, very hard as I continued to move forward. Now, I needed God's direct protection. I truly felt he was right there with me, right by my side. This was the most dangerous that I had ever been in. An explosion happened on my right, and I saw the other gunner go down. It was a really big explosion, and it took out one Marine infantry also. I wonder what it was because it was so big. I continued to move with the last of the Marines. There were only a few of us left now, maybe ten or so in our section of the hill, not many out of the fifty-two in this platoon at the beginning of the attack. I wondered if Corporal Hall was still with us. I hoped he was OK. I prayed for him too. Suddenly, it appeared to be over. We were at the top and there was no enemy on the reverse slope. We threw grenades into the last of the bunkers on the top just to make sure. There were a few wounded enemies, which we took prisoner. None had surrendered though. They all fought until they could not fight anymore. They were very good and brave men, and they did their best. Their families and their country should have been very proud of them. This enemy was a part of, or maybe all of, the NVA 257th Regiment, one of their best. It looked like they were going to need a lot of new men for the 257th, or perhaps they just would retire the unit as the U.S. Army did in similar cases (so I have heard). Somehow, though, I thought we would meet on the 257th again one day. We had been fighting this unit for a long time now in different parts of the Quang Tri Province. They seemed to, and I heard they did, follow my unit around to specifically engage us.

I looked around for Corporal Hall but did not see him. Maybe he got separated from us or perhaps wounded. I wondered how the second and third platoons did. I hoped for better than us. Later I learned that there were nine of the first platoon left, second platoon had eight lefts, and third had only five. Only one corpsman made it and seventeen weapons platoons with and thirteen left in the company command group for a total of fifty-three left out of two hundred fifty-four that we started with that day. Most of us did die or were wounded this day in March 1968.

I slumped against a bunker and realized how tired I was. We had done it! It was a very costly win though. I looked my body over to see if I had wounds. I looked down at my feet and was actually surprised they were both there. I do not know why I was surprised, but I was. I looked at my legs, my arms, and my chest. All was OK. Just very dirty and covered with blood from others; my utilities were almost all red from blood and spattered with mud, still damp in places from the blood. One thing seemed funny; I was not thirsty, not at all. That was not normal for me.

Vietnam War 1972, Bruno Barbey

Chapter 7

March 6, 17:35:05

I was very happy we made it. I looked around at those there with me and saw none of my men. I was missing the whole squad. None made it to the top with me. Most had died; a few were carried down to the helicopter medevac area by the corpsmen and taken to Da Nang or to the carrier offshore and on to Japan. I was not sure which made it, and which died. I only knew there was no one with me now. It was a very sad and lonely feeling. My squad was gone; all of it.

We started blowing up all the bunkers with C4 blasting compound. The C4 worked well for this. A very small amount of C4 caused a big explosion. The difficulty we had with this was that to make it blow you needed a smaller explosion inside of it, a fuse. We had caps with electronic switches but not many of those, so we had to use lit fuses attached to caps then stuff these caps into the gray claylike C4. The fuse was a bit unreliable; caps and C4 were good. Because of the moisture and the water, we went through in the swamps and rice paddies, the lit fuses did not always work. If they were damp, they would burn unreliably, sometimes very fast so you had to run like hell after you lit them, and other times very slowly or they would seem to go out completely and then suddenly start burning again, maybe real fast, then go out again, very unpredictable. Months earlier, we were destroying old enemy bunkers, which we came across on a search-and-destroy mission. We had one bunker where we placed the charge with a very slow fuse. I waited in a bomb crater with the Marine who lit it, but it did not go off. We waited at least five minutes, and then I told him to go check it. We could not just leave it because it might fall into the hands of the enemy. He cautiously approached the bunker, ready to duck. He got up to the bunker and peered in. Just at that moment, it exploded right in his face; totally destroying the bunker and throwing him up in the air ten feet and back twenty. I got up to him, expecting to find him dead. He was alive and very dazed. He could not hear at all. I could see no wounds but was concerned that there might be more serious internal damage, so I got a corpsman, and we put him on medevac. I thought he would be back in a few days after they checked him out, but I never saw him again. It must have been serious.

We stayed at the top of the hill for about forty-five minutes and then were ordered to reassemble in the medevac area. We left the top of the hill after double checking that we retrieved all of our dead. It was strangely quiet as we left. It seemed funny. We went through so much to take the hill then we just walked away from it. I guess the idea was the enemy could rebuild there if they wanted, but we would come back, take it again, and kill them. We were United States Marines, the best fighting force in the world. If they wanted me to come back and take the hill again later, I would, without question, just as each man left would, and we would all comeback with a lot more experience behind us next time.

We moved into a clearing, about one-fourth of the way down the hill; helicopters were landing picking up the dead. The wounded had already been removed and were now in Da Nang. That was a blessing. If we could get them on a medevac fast enough after they were wounded, they would have a great chance of survival. Usually there were corpsmen on the helicopters to take care of the men right away, and sometimes there was a doctor. Once I even saw a doctor and a nurse. I was concerned that they were in a battle area but so glad that my men were getting the very best of care as fast as possible. In the field, we could not do much for them, especially the seriously wounded. We would administer morphine and compress the wound with a dressing to slow the bleeding, but that was about all we could do. Bleeding was the big problem especially with the heat of Vietnam. Often it was impossible to control the bleeding. I feel we lost most of our men from bleeding out rather than fatal damage to body parts. This happened when we could not get to them right away to compress the wound because of battlefield conditions. In other wars like in Korea, the cold actually helped to stop the bleeding, but they had a different problem as there was not much helicopter medevac available. So even though they did not bleed as badly, it was harder to get them to the hospital fast.

The dead were arranged in a long line, lying next to each other, side by side, covered by a poncho. Just their boots were visible. I walked down the line and stopped. I looked at the boots that stuck out from the poncho. They were not different than anyone else's boots, except I knew it was Hall. I knew then that he did not make it from a wound or just off in another sector. I knew he was gone. I was sad for him and felt very alone. I stayed with him until they moved his body to the chopper. I found the one man left from his squad and asked him if he knew what happened. He said, "Yes, I was there." He said, "It was just before the last attack up the hill when we were going down the trenches and throwing grenades in the bunkers. Corporal Hall was just behind the lead man. Suddenly, an enemy jumped out in front of them, fired, and killed the Marine in front. Hall, instead of firing, reached out to the man falling in front of him to catch him. The enemy then fired and shot Hall. I then fired and killed the enemy. I checked Hall and the other Marine, and they were both dead." This did sound like Hall. He was a caring and basically gentle human being. I am sure his instinct was to reach out for his falling Marine. I wish he would have fired, but I understand. Not everything is about war. I miss Hall, still to this day.

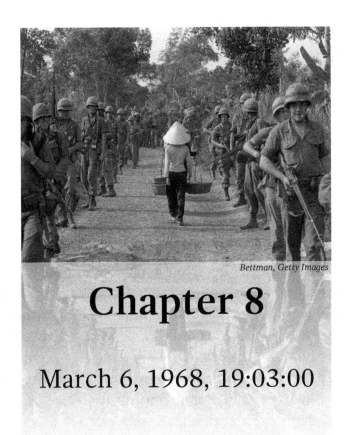

Bettman, Getty Images

Chapter 8

March 6, 1968, 19:03:00

My thirst was coming back, which I consider a good thing now, but I was not as thirsty as before and the afternoon; moving toward evening was cooling a little. So, I was probably going to make it until we got back to the perimeter. That is, if we went back tonight. I knew there was a possibility we would dig in where we were for the night. I hoped we were going back. The last of the choppers came and went. I was wishing one of them had dropped some water, but it didn't look like it. I was thinking about starting to dig a fighting hole for the night when we got the word we go back. This surprised me a little because it was beginning to get dark, and we did not usually move after dark except to set up ambushes. I was glad though; I wanted to get back. We moved on down the hill. In the dusk, it did not look like the same hill. It was so quiet now except for the sound of us moving through the jungle, but even that was quiet. We came to the base of the hill and started moving across the rice paddies. Got water! As we entered the rice paddies, I immediately stuck my canteen into the murky water and filled a canteen. I dropped a halizone water purification tablet into the canteen and told myself I had to wait at least twenty minutes before I could drink. It took at least that long to kill all the bad parasites in the water. I was thinking that by then we would be back in the perimeter, but just in case something happens, and we do not, at least I would have some water. Well, it turned out, I could not wait that long and drank after only about five minutes. I did pay the price for that. It was the second time I paid that price. The first time, however, was the worst. That was what I talked about in the prologue. After we finished that march in the heat, we arrived at a perimeter that had been hit badly the night before. That is why we were pushing to get there so hard. I did not know why, but I knew it was important. When we got there, I could see why. There were dead enemies lying everywhere. The machine gun position we took over had taken many hits. The machine gunners inside did not even want to get out until it was time for them to leave. They said it was hell. It did look bad, and they had no defenses set up. No barbed wire, no claymores, no trip wires, just them facing the jungle. They had those eyes that just sort of stared out at you, big, just kind of looking through you and not at you. Then I knew why we had to reinforce them (actually take over the position); it did not look like they could handle another assault. At any rate, as we came up to their perimeter from our long hot march, we formed a nice stream, flowing nice fresh water from which we all filled our canteens. I dropped halizone in just in case but could not wait long before I drank. It was so good and cold. Later when I started getting sick, someone told me that there were several dead enemies just upstream from where we filled our canteens, and that they fouled the water, and now everyone was getting sick. Oh, was I sick. The next day I had to go out and help lay barbed wire, and I nearly passed out. I was so dizzy and had such bad diarrhea I could not even tell I was going to the bathroom. I was a mess. I fell asleep on watch the second night there because of the illness. The line watch banged me on the back of the helmet with his rifle so hard that I went rolling down the hill in front of me. My head was ringing from the blow, but it already hurt so bad from the illness, it really did not matter. He said that if I fell asleep again, he would put a bullet into me. I think he meant it. We did actually have to ask permission to shoot anyone who fell asleep at night. They say there would be a court martial, however, that would result in you being charged twenty-eight cents for the bullet you used. I never heard of this actually happening, but they were very serious about you staying awake. Later when I became a squad leader and did the line watch, I threatened many people in exactly the same way. It was absolutely required that you stay awake at night, one person in each fighting position. I felt bad that I fell asleep and did the rest of the watch standing up and many more after that. I realized that after a very hard day, it was difficult to stay awake for all of us, but we had to do it. Many times, I fell asleep while standing, and it hurts really bad and wakes you up when you fall on your knees from a standing position. Later I developed a technique of making coffee under my poncho at night, which if done correctly, the making and drinking of a cup of coffee could take exactly three hours, the duration of each watch. By doing this and keeping busy, I did not fall asleep. The way this was done is as follows: slowly open a can of bread or one of the smaller c-ration cans. I would cut the top completely off with the small c-ration can openers provided. I would then cut holes in the side of the base of the can. This was the stove. I would then take a tall can and take the top of one end and clean it out and pour coffee, sugar, cream, and water into it. I would then pull off a small amount of C4 blasting compound and roll it into a small ball about the diameter of a quarter. I would put that in my stove and light it. This stuff would burn very hot for about five minutes. I would then put the coffee on top of the stove and let it boil. The C4 put off a lot of heat, so if it was a cold night, it would warm up the whole inside of the poncho. This part, the preparation of the coffee, usually took about an hour and a half. I did it very slowly to keep me busy and use up the time. The last hour or so was dedicated to sipping the very hot coffee. If I needed to rewarm the coffee, it was easy, just a little more C4. This worked very well to keep me awake. I told others about it too so that they could stay awake, and of course, through this process, you needed to keep a very watchful eye out for the enemy and never, never expose any light from the burning C4. We got only two three-hour periods of sleep a night with that broken into by two three-hour periods of standing watch. When my watch was over, I fell immediately asleep and would sleep soundly for the next three hours, practically no matter what happened. Often there would be an artillery barrage from the enemy; I might wake up briefly and would go right back to sleep. Once Vought asked me how the hell, I could sleep though that. I smiled and said I was very tired. He said that I must have been. I asked him if they really were coming to get me up. He smiled and said he would.

I looked around at the other Marines coming off the hill as we moved into the rice paddy, and they did look as though they had been through a major battle. Many had bandages around their heads or arms or legs. Our uniforms were dirty, bloody, and torn. Some men were missing helmets. We looked pretty rag-tag and beat up. We were about ten meters into the rice paddies. I was wondering if the Lieutenant made it when I hear someone hell out "Corporal Hagedorn!" I looked to my left; about fifteen meters away was the lieutenant. He had made it! He yelled, "Get these men online." I do not know why, but I had a sudden flash of anger. I was carrying my rifle pointing down at the rice paddy but with my finger on the trigger, safety off as always, always ready, and without really thinking, just pulled the trigger and put three rounds into the ground. The bullets must have been very close to my foot. The spray from the water splashed all the way up into my face. This was impulsive and crazy; I know, but I needed a release, I think. I immediately yelled as loud as I could, "Get online!" I did not really expect the men to obey the command for some reason, probably because we were all so tired, so I was surprised when I saw them get online, a perfect line too, with it as straight as could be. I yelled again, "Look smart!" And they all stood straight and began to look like Marines again, with pride, almost marching through the rice paddy. Then one of them began to sing the Mickey Mouse song, just one voice in the quiet evening, a good voice I thought. Others joined in, then others, and finally I joined in. We all sang; we sang it over and over, as loud as we could, all the way back home. Coming up to the perimeter in the dark, singing, they must have thought we were crazy.

Our company was now the size of a platoon. We rested for three days, the few of us that were left, and then a new sergeant walked up to us. He was the replacement for Hobbes. He said casually, "OK girls, we are going for a little stroll, not a big deal but just to get you all back in the saddle again so mount up." He seemed to be a good enough guy, but this was the first time I saw him. Well, now we had fifty-four, and that was important. Our numbers were increasing again. Since I had no machine gunners left, I was given the second squad to lead temporarily until we got some more Marines in. I did feel scared as we left the relative security of the perimeter but told myself this was just a little stroll then back before dark. Not a big deal. To the north of our perimeter was the DMZ, a three-mile-wide defoliated area known as No Man's Land. They kept this area defoliated by occasionally coming by and dropping Agent Orange on it. This did work well to keep the jungle from growing, but a corpsman did warn me to not drink the water from the bomb craters here because they were bound to have a lot of Agent Orange in them. I asked why, and what else would I drink, there is no fresh water here, and we do not get supplied with any? He said, "I am not sure, but anything that stops plants from growing probably is not good to drink, and I think may result in health problems later in life." He then added "It may not matter though. Most of us would not be alive in six months anyway." Well, that part was correct. As long as it did not kill us immediately, then the future probably did not matter too much. I drank the crater water a lot because there was no fresh water. It seemed that if they brought in a chopper, it would be carrying ammo first, and then maybe some food and then taking out our dead and wounded, but never fresh, safe water. A funny story though. Our new Lieutenant Hawkins came by early one morning after a month or so in Vietnam carrying a five-gallon jerry can, when I was shaving. It was required that we shave every morning, even if we did nothing else. He asked me how much fresh water I had. He said, "Not crater water, fresh water." I said, "I have about an eighth of a canteen left, Sir." This was my precious water, very valuable. I would pour out just a little bit every morning to brush my teeth with and then shave. It was the luxury of the day. Just a little in the bottom of my canteen cup to take care of all my clean up. I used crater water to wash my hands and face. He said simply said, "Give it to me." I did. I wondered what was up and have to admit I thought the worst of the lieutenant. I thought he was gathering it for himself. He went to each fighting hole and took whatever they had. Most had none. A few days passed, and I was talking to the radioman and said, "Hey, how about the lieutenant, I thought he was a pretty good guy until he came along and took all our fresh water." The radioman laughed and said, "You didn't hear what he did with that?" I said I thought he used it for himself. The radioman laughed again and said, "You're going to love this. He took the can in to the command post and came up behind the battalion commander as he sat over his maps studying our next big, planned attack and dumped it all over him. The commander was furious and demanded to know why Hawkins would do such a thing to a superior officer. Hawkins said that he thought the commander might enjoy a shower and to cool off a little with the last of his men's fresh water." Picture that, a platoon boot lieutenant dumping the water all over a high Rank Major. He was right. I did enjoy that and still laugh when I think about it. That commander must have been so pissed off. I kept laughing and said, "Well, that explains why within the next hour I was up in one of the observation bunkers with Hall and saw a chopper coming directly for us. I could see it was carrying something underneath with the binoculars but could not make out what it was until it got close—something big and black hanging from it." Hall said, "I think it's a water bag." He was right. I little later, we were taking turns going with our canteens (all our canteens) to get fresh water. It was like a party. That was the first time and just about the only time we had fresh water to drink. Fresh water was not the only thing that was not available besides ponchos; after the first month or so, my underwear began to just shred apart. I asked one of the old timers when we would be resupplied with underwear. He laughed and said, "We will be lucky to get socks. You can forget about underwear. No one has ever gotten any once the ones you arrived with rotted off. You won't see any, so forget that idea." He was right; we never did get any in the field and sometimes had trouble getting utility pants when they started to fall off. I had never in my life not had underwear and did not like it now, but it was just one more thing I had to get used to. I told myself this is not a big deal and just get used to it. It did not matter anyway. I was about to go for nine months without taking a bath or even removing my utility pants except to change them once in the next nine months to ones that were not all ripped up. Not having underwear was bad, but the ponchos kept us warm at night, and not having one of those certainly made it uncomfortable. I would curl up into a little ball, in the fetal position in the bottom of the fox hole I dug or in the bunker and try to warm myself with my breath on those really cold winter nights, and on the DMZ, it did get cold. I would unzip my flak jacket a little and breathe into the opening, warming my chest. My back and legs got really cold, but my chest stayed pretty warm this way. I was always out of a poncho because I would give mine to a seriously wounded Marine or use it to carefully cover one of my dead. I kept promising myself I would not do this again because it was necessary for me to keep so that I was able to perform, but somehow, when someone was hit, I would always give it to him no matter how much I promised myself to keep it. My dead did not need it (I would tell myself), but when it came time, I felt it was necessary to cover them. I kept telling myself I would not do it again because I needed it so badly but always did. Sacrifice!

I lost my tooth because the corpsmen would not medevac me to take care of it, and I did not really blame them. There were definitely more important issues at hand. It started hurting about two months after I got there, third from the back, left bottom one. It was very painful, and my jaw was swollen up. One day, after a bad battle, it hurt so badly. I again asked a corpsman for a medevac. He pointed at the battalion commander and said to ask him and smiled like he thought I would not have the guts to do it. I did. I walked over to him. He was standing in the middle of a men lying around him, both dead and wounded from the battle we just went through. I asked, and he was silent for a second. I thought he might explode in rage; he just to a long look around at the men lying everywhere then out in front of us where the entire dead enemy lay. He answered then in an almost soft voice, "I cannot do that. I need every man left, here, but I will have a corpsman check on you. You will just have to handle the pain." I said, "Yes, Sir." I felt better and was glad I asked and knew I was going to have to endure the pain. The corpsman did check on me and did what he could. It took nearly four months before the tooth completely died and the pain stopped. One day, suddenly, the pain was gone. It felt so good, and I was so happy. One of the men joked but perhaps in half-truth that they did not want to fix the tooth if I was just going to die in a few more weeks anyway. I thought that there was some truth here, plus I knew they needed to keep me in the field to fight. As the commander said, they needed everyone then, and they did. It was very difficult for anyone to get a medevac unless in serious condition. Even the lightly wounded were bandaged up and immediately returned to the field. Only the seriously wounded and dead would be leaving now; the rest of us were here to stay and either win or die. We knew that, and it did motivate us to fight hard, because this was it, no other options. We were also motivated though because we were United States Marines and very proud of that. A lot of civilians criticized us for this pride, saying that it was wrong, a false pride, but we did not listen to them; we listened to our hearts and fought for each other and loved each other, a deeper love, and a more special love than these citizens will ever know. We fought for the country that seemed to be rejecting us because we believed in the correctness of what we were doing, and even if many in the country were against us, we had each other, which we loved.

My men would come down with malaria, and I would have to wait until their temperatures got to one hundred four degrees. This was high, and I knew brain damage occurs at one hundred six, so I would watch them very closely, taking their temperatures every half hour until they hit the mark. Then I would get to the corpsman and a medevac as fast as possible. Toward the end of my tour, the corpsmen did not even bother to check their temperatures when I brought them up. One just said, "We know you know what you are doing," and radioed for the medevac. I came down with malaria also. I was sick for about a week and missed patrols for a day when my fever was at its worst, but for some reason, it did not get really bad. I did not hit that magic mark of one hundred four, so I remained in the field through it. I did take the malaria pill once a week as required and that may be why I did not get it worse, because I would take mine. It was bad but never got really bad. They say once you have it, it can sporadically reoccur through the rest of your life, and at times over the years, it felt like I had it again sometimes, but I could not be sure that it was not just a bad case of flu. I was told that once you had malaria, it stayed in your blood for the rest of your life, and that I should not donate blood. Don't know for sure if that is true but have not donated blood, just in case. Every Sunday morning (and that was how I knew what day was Sunday), a corpsman would make his rounds giving each of us a pill and standing by until he was sure we swallowed it. He would have us open our mouths to make sure we did swallow it and not just hold it there and spit it out after they left. At first this surprised me that some tried not take the pill, but as I became aware of the intense combat we were subjected to over time, I could understand why some would rather have malaria and get sent to the hospital. I did not want to get malaria and would rather stay in the field than sit in a hospital. I had asked a Marine why in the world they would not want to take it, and he simply said that many would prefer to have malaria and sit in a hospital then face constant death in a battlefield. I do not blame them but was surprised by this.

I heard that the same went for rat bites. I heard that they gave daily shots in the stomach for rabies for two weeks, and it was very painful. I was told that some guys opted for that over remaining in constant combat, but I never saw or heard of anyone in our unit doing that. Most perimeters that we held were OK, but some of the older ones, ones that had been around through years of fighting where Marines or South Vietnamese had been stationed for long periods of time, were crawling with rats, and I do not mean little rats. I mean gigantic rats, almost the size of cats. These things were large, larger than any I have ever seen before or since. I asked why they were so large, and a guy said it was from all the protein. I said, "What protein?" He said, "Protein from the dead bodies." I did not want to believe this, but I do think it was true. They were so large that sometimes when they were out in front of us in the barbed wire moving around, they would rattle the wire and our tin cans, and we would alert as if enemy zappers were crawling through. I am sure I killed many rats with my grenade throwing at night but better safe than sorry. One night I woke up to the movement of one of these large rats sitting on my chest. I was in a bunker, not a deep one, but it was well fortified with sandbags and even a steel plate across the top. Through the opening where our machine gun sat, I could see one of our flares slowly drifting down on a small parachute. In the light, I could see the rat sitting there, up a little on its haunches a little, a very big rat, and that is why I thought it was the puppy when I was first waking up. It was about as big and heavy as the puppy, but then I remembered I let Jones have it for the night. The rat was just looking at me, staring me right in the eyes less than a foot from my face. I think he was actually testing me and seemed to be communicating with me in his own rat like way. This was not the puppy that a tank crew man gave me a couple days before. The tank was behind my fighting position, and I had said hi to the crew a few times after we occupied the machine gun bunker. Often tank guys were a little snobby, but these guys were friendly enough. One of the guys came up to me just before they pulled back to Da Nang and offered me the puppy, indicating his officer would not let him keep it anymore. I took it (it was so cute) but knew our officers would not let us keep it either. I decided that at least we could have it for a while, and then I would pass it along, and it did improve all of our morale. It was a really cute little puppy that just loved to give puppy licks. We all fell in love with it, and everyone who came by wanted to hold it. Anyway, I woke up gently, thinking it was the puppy on my chest, but it was not. So, what to do with this rat sitting on my chest, staring me in the eyes? I decided the best thing to do was just go back to sleep and let the rat sit there if he wanted to; after all he was here first. I closed my eyes and started to drift off again and felt the rat slowly move off my chest and heard him go back into the sandbags just above my head. I knew that if he wanted to, he could bit me at any time. I feel we had a meeting of minds, and something of a friendship was established. I had decided a truce might be the best approach here. I think we became something of friends over the next few days before we left that area. He pretty much just left me alone, and I left him alone. I did spot him a couple times as he casually crawled around the sandbags, but I made no attempt to injure him. We were able to keep the puppy about a week before the lieutenant noticed it and told me I had to get rid of it. One day I was carrying it inside my flak jacket with the jacket partially unzipped, just enough so his head could stick out. The little puppy would cuddle down in there and be safe. At one point, we passed by a fairly populated village, and the children came out to see our parade, to ask for candy and with some trying to sell us "dien cai dau" cigarettes. These were cigarettes made from black hash, a very powerful narcotic, one dollar for one cigarette. Yes, there were a lot of drugs in Vietnam. I never once tried anything though. I figured I already had my hands full without being stoned out too. One of the little boys noticed the puppy I was carrying and immediately "offered me" ten dollars for it. I was astounded. I thought, how wonderful, this little boy wants this puppy so bad he is willing to give a lot of money for it, and in Vietnam then, ten dollars was a lot of money. I nearly gave it to him but was too attached to it. I said to the Marine near me, "Isn't that nice, this little boy wants a puppy." Again, I had it wrong evidently. The guy laughed and said, "He wants to buy it so they can eat it. Here, dog meat is good meat." I learned that what he said was true, and we never saw any dogs just running around. They all went to the dinner table as soon as there was a little meat on them. He pointed that out to me too. I felt sorry for the people. In America, we have so much food, so much meat that this would never be a thought, but here, it was a basic necessity. After a couple days, I found someone with another tank group and gave them the puppy. I wonder what happened to the puppy over time and sure hope it did not wind up as dinner. Who knows, maybe someone was able to get it back to the United States perhaps in one of the big C-130 airplanes. That is a great thought.

For my full tour in Vietnam, I drank from swamps, rice paddies, and bomb craters, all of which had heavy doses of Agent Orange (not to mention visible bugs, parasites, twigs, and mud) and seldom had fresh water. I feel that drinking all the Agent Orange did have later effects on me and my yet-to-be-born children. Three years ago, I lost my twelve-year-old daughter Celeste to a rare form of cancer, Ewing's sarcoma; my little boy (Richard Jr.) has suffered from severe epileptic seizures since birth; and my oldest daughter, Carol was born with a displaced hip and could not walk correctly. Diana is now suffering from emotional problems and is currently in an institution in Utah. I thought perhaps Alexander, my youngest, was going to get through with no issues, but a brain problem has recently developed. It seems that I had not seen the last of the war when I left there in June 1968. It has continued to haunt me all my life, not only in dreams but in real life as I am sure it has all who fought with me. That is, if they were lucky enough to even get out of there alive, they must still face the nightmares and realities of life for a Vietnam Marine combat veteran. Losing Celeste was even more difficult than all the combat I survived in Vietnam. It tore me and my family apart and hurt worse than anything I have ever been through. To watch that little innocent girl suffers, and die was absolutely the worst thing that could have happened to me. The Veterans Administration (VA) maintains there is no connection between these types of congenital defects and Agent Orange, and I feel they are wrong. They are not helping me with any of these issues, and they should. They continue to avoid the issues with Agent Orange even though there is overwhelming evidence that it has caused many problems for many families of returning Vietnam veteran. They now, finally, after thirty-five years have recognized it as a problem but only look at the veteran and not his family. Currently, the children receive no VA coverage yet suffer from the damage unless the veteran is declared 100 percent disabled. This is wrong. PTSD has also finally been recognized as a valid issue among veterans but had remained on the back seat since the very first wars that America fought. The VA was unwilling to accept the idea of PTSD over the decades, and so many men suffered from it. Now they accept it as if it was a fact always known (as it was) but had resisted helping our veterans through all these years and all of their suffering. I think many more would be alive today if this had been acknowledged decades ago, and certainly the families of these veterans deserve compensation for all the injuries they too have suffered. There was a time when men who went to war returned with honor and were given property and were celebrated and placed automatically in senate positions and assisted for the rest of their lives because of the service they rendered. Should this not be so for the combat veterans of today? Should their families not be taken care of entirely because so many gave their life defending this country and help others? I think so. They are asked to do so much, the ultimate sacrifice, and then return to a worse struggle than the average person has to go through. We must struggle with the memories of combat and the guilt that we have survived, and our very best friends are now lying in their graves.

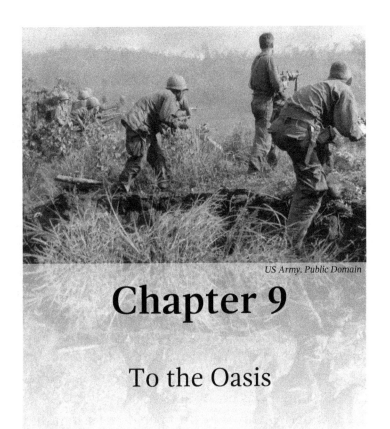

US Army. Public Domain

Chapter 9

To the Oasis

So off we went, over the barren waist land of the DMZ that looked like the landscape of the moon with the entire large bomb craters, on our little day stroll, heading for our turn around point that we called the Oasis. As we circled around one bomb crater, a Marine pointed up to the skeleton remains of a dead tree. Stuck in the tree, and actually pasted to the tree, about ten feet off the ground was an enemy soldier. He still had his helmet, cartridge belt, and all his gear on. He was just hanging there as if he had been placed there. When one of the bombs went off, it must have caught him just right to plant him there. It was probably one of the "Arch Light" operations that were flown very often and especially over the DMZ at night to catch enemy troop movements. From what we were looking at, it did look like this operation was successful and caught them in the open. In these operations, the B52s would drop hundreds of thousand-pound bombs from very high altitude. The altitude was so high you could not even hear them, and they were long gone even before their bombs began to hit. These bombs were big, very big, and I know because one morning one of them landed in our parameter about four fox holes from mine. It was early morning, and I was shaving. I heard a whistle but not like the sound of artillery, just a long steady whistle. I looked up into the air in the direction of the sound. It was overcast so at first, I saw nothing, and then it parted the clouds. It was a very large B52 bomb, and it was landing right on us. I lay on the ground but knew it was too close. I knew that lying on the ground would not do much good. I knew how big this was and could hear and feel it strike the ground. I was pretty sure this was it for me, and I was also wondering why they dropped it on us; it must have been a mistake. I waited for the explosion, probably a delayed explosion, so the bomb could work its way into the ground to blow up a deep bunker. I waited several minutes, no explosion. A dud? I walked over to where it hit. It looked like a perfectly dug well, going deep into the earth. The lieutenant walked up and said that it must have not quite released from the B52 on their bomb run up north and shook loose over us as the planes headed back to their air base. One night, we stood on a hill miles away (after the whole battalion had moved out of the parameter and walked for half a day to get far enough away) and watched the orange fire explosions rake across the land, one after another. It was an awesome sight to see, feel, and hear. I would not like to be on the receiving end of that. Even from our safe position on a hillside watching the Arch Light, the concussion was tremendous. We could not be anywhere near when these operations took place. Even miles away, the ground shook under our feet, and we could feel the concussion hit us wave after wave as the orange mushroom fireballs appeared in the distance, one after another seemingly endless.

The Oasis was about midway across the DMZ or approximately one and a half miles from our perimeter and pretty much directly north of our position. We zigzagged a little (mainly because of the craters) as we went but pretty much headed straight for the Oasis. It was close enough to see from our perimeter and stood out as the only green patch in an area that really did look like the face of the moon, complete with all the craters. The Oasis was an area two to three acres in size, fed by underground streams, so no matter how much Agent Orange they dropped on that, it would not go away. I had been there a few times on patrol and would always fill my canteens there, knowing the water was good and fresh. I was actually looking forward to the visit and thought yes, a nice little day trip, get fresh water then back to the nice safe perimeter. Good deal! A lot of my fears from the previous fighting were relieved as we moved on. Everything was fine, and it was a good day.

The small squad I lead was the first to enter the Oasis, and a chill went through my body as the Marine near me suddenly stopped and pointed at the edge of the Oasis vegetation. The very first thing I saw was a large fresh fox hole, the dirt still damp from digging. Around the hole were an NVA shovel, an enemy soldier's helmet, food (rice), and canteen. The dirt was fresh. They were just here; they must still be here a little further back in the Oasis. This was not good. Not only were they here, but they were regulars (because of the equipment scattered around), and immediately I understood; they were a force, a large force moving to the south to fight, and they got caught by the approaching daylight and decided to hold up here for the day hoping to begin the movement again after dark. We just walked into it. We caught them by surprise, but they would be regrouping by now and getting ready to come at us with the idea of total annihilation. I knew we were in real trouble. There were not many of us, and I knew there must have been a lot of them. I glanced behind me and knew we could not leave without getting mowed down. It was open ground for over a mile, and we would never make it. We would just have to fight it out here and now, and I knew it would not be good. I was very scared and prayed to the Holy Ghost thinking that soon I would be seeing him. I prayed for the men with me and thought it was unfair that we survived the battle three days ago on March the 6, only to die here and now today. The more I thought, the more I knew we were way outnumbered (it turned out to be more than a full regiment of enemy North Vietnam Army regulars [NVA] that got stopped here and that we would fight today). That was over two thousand enemies against fifty-four. The odds were very bad. It reminded me of the old joke where two Marines are completely surround by enemy when they wake up, and then one Marine confidently says to the other, "Well, they're not going to get away this time." I knew we were going to have to fight it out, and I did not expect we were going to win. We did have some points on our side. We had all survived the intense fighting a few days earlier, so we were experienced and knew how to fight. Of the full company, I was with pretty much the best of the fighters, and just maybe we had a chance. We were way outnumbered though, and the enemy had a chance to watch us approach, so they knew exactly how strong we were. I expect they were thinking they would make quick work of us. That is pretty much what I was thinking too. I realized I only had about fifteen minutes to live, maybe thirty outside. I prayed again.

We lay in a line about two meters into the jungle of the Oasis. The enemy started raking us down our line, with heavy mortar fire. They knew exactly where we were and delivered very accurate fire. This lasted for five minutes or so, and then the radioman ran by yelling that we had to move into the Oasis more and scatter a little so they could not just rake us with the mortars. He said to me as he passed that we had already lost seven; one of the seven was my Kit Carson, the X North Vietnam Army (NVA) regular who had been captured and trained and converted to U.S. Marine. He had actually been sent to Monterey California to the U.S. Defense Language Institute to learn English then put through a Marine boot camp (not easy to get through). He was assigned to my unit because he had fought with the enemy here, against us, and knew the area. I became his friend. None of the other Marines liked him because he was former enemy (a turn coat, not even loyal to his own army), but I knew the United States put a lot of money into him and that he knew the area. I did not completely trust him and would keep him close in firefights at first to make sure he was not killed by one of our men, and that he did not kill any of our men. After a while, I trusted him completely and the men began to accept him a little, but most did not like it; that I was friendly to him and even got mad about it, but I told them it was necessary to get his information. One time we were in the perimeter, and we had to report to the CP for briefing, and as we were walking, he took my hand. This was strange, but that was the way they were and their custom of friendship. I felt uncomfortable, especially in front of the men but did not pull away. I held his hand as a friend and then I trusted him. He did save my life by shooting an enemy on the field just before the enemy could shoot me. Also, he would do field interrogation of those we captured to try to find out what the enemy was planning. Where they were currently, and were they getting ready to attack? So, I kept him close most of the time. He could smell the enemy before we knew they were there and even before the dogs could. He once pointed out the barrel of an enemy machine gun hidden from view in front of us, sticking out of a very well-camouflaged bunker. We got it before it got any of us. I am glad we had him. He had become a real Marine, even though he was not accepted by others. I was sorry to lose him and missed him. He had become a friend and fought closely with me on the sixth of March. His name was Tam.

We had to move forward! I knew he was right, but I was not looking forward to moving "into them." I knew it would get bad, and there would be hand-to-hand fighting before this was over. I yelled to fix bayonets. The word was passed down the line, and we moved forward. We attacked—this small group of men against so many. After close fighting and some hand-to-hand fighting, we secured several bunkers.

Two more Marines died in this process when some enemy counter attacked and jumped into their temporary fighting position. I went to their hole. There were two dead Americans and three dead NVAs, one with a bayonet in his chest. The situation was getting more desperate. The jungle here was dense. There were just too many of them, and they were moving in fast and throwing grenades all around us. Bursts of AK47 lashing out from the jungle in front of us. Tracer rounds with the bright red trailing streamer, like a laser beam, screaming past our helmets, smashing into the ground around us, slicing through the vegetation, cutting it in half; grenade explosions going off all around us. One grenade landed right next to me one foot away, on my right, right between me and another Marine. I yelled to him to roll to get away from it before it went off. We both did a roll away from the grenade, and strangely it did not go off. As we rolled, I noticed that he had trouble rolling because of a LAW he was carrying (along with a lot of other equipment), and that gave me an idea. Even though we had strict orders not to fire the LAW except at an enemy tank and only at an enemy tank, I decided those orders would soon not matter anyway—after we were all dead. I thought maybe I could hit the enemy command post with it. I could tell and could guess where it was located. If I could get close enough, maybe I could disrupt the attack. I had only fired the LAW once before in advanced infantry training, and I remembered the instructor saying to read the instructions carefully. I laughed (to myself) at the time, thinking sure thing. I am in the middle of combat with a tank coming my way, and I will just sit down and read the instructions like nothing is going on. I knew all the rules regarding firing one of these like making sure no one was behind me (the back blast could seriously injure someone), but I did not remember the steps to arm it. There were four steps, and each had to be performed in the correct order. So, I sat and read the directions. When I thought I had it set to fire, I squatted up; estimated where I heard the mortars and determined to fire just in front of them hoping the enemy command post (CP) would be there. I thought this was likely as that is how we usually set up; the CP just in front of the mortars so that the CP could help direct their fire. I was ready, estimating it to be about four hundred meters away and a little to the left of direct forward, slightly northwest but more north than northwest. I pulled the trigger, and nothing happened. I thought that maybe the LAW was bad. It was muddy from going through a lot of swamps, but I remembered the instruction and the instructor saying these things are very reliable and will always fire. Still, it was very dirty, and a bit dented up from many hours of being carried through the jungle, but I was counting on what the instructor said: "These were very reliable even with a lot of abuse." I sat down and read the directions again. I found the step I missed and was pretty sure it would fire now. I prepared to fire again and took a quick glance around and noticed another squad leader not too far away to my left, the other Corporal in our platoon; we were the only two lefts at this point. He had a LAW too. He saw what I was doing and decided to join in. I waited a few seconds while he got his ready. He was fast. He did not read the instructions and was ready to fire in a few seconds. With hand signals, I indicated that I would fire a little short from the sound of the position of the enemy mortars, and that he was to fire a little long. I prayed that one of us would find the mark. He understood and nodded in the affirmative. We fired him a little ahead of mine. The explosions were very, very big. I had forgotten how powerful these weapons were. I knew by the sound of things we had done some significant damage. The mortars were silenced. The rifle and machine gunfire all but lifted. The enemy seemed to stop attacking us almost immediately. I was excited that this might have worked. I knew that without the CP and the leader, the Rank and file usually did not function well; unlike the Marine Corps whose fighting ability was still excellent even without leaders; every man was trained to fight on his own when necessary. The enemy needed to have leadership, or their functional fighting ability failed. With the loss of leadership, they would break and run. We soon found out that we did take out the regiment CP; the enemy was in disarray and fleeing across the open fields on the back (north side) side of the Oasis, the whole enemy regiment. There was a small propeller plane that came into view. It was a spotter plane for jets and artillery to call in support. The pilot was actually leaning out of the window firing a carbine at the enemy as they ran. He radioed to our lieutenant that there were hundreds running to the north, and they were sitting ducks (well running ducks in this case). He was picking them off one by one. I later heard that the pilot was our Marine Corps Ed McMahon who later in life became famous as the announcer for the Jonny Carson Late Night Show on TV. Ed was a Marine pilot and a very good Marine. He was taking fire from the ground but continued his assault.

The whole enemy regiment was routed. The 81MM mortars for our perimeter started firing on the fleeing enemy. The pilot radioed that we were killing hundreds of enemies. The jets then arrived and finished off the enemy regiment with napalm, heat bombs, and jet machine gunfire.

They were easy targets as they ran across the open ground trying to get back to the jungles in the north for protection. I was thinking that could have been us trying to get away from them. Our job was done; we just listened to all the explosions and machine gunfire coming from the jets with an occasional enemy AK47 opening up, and when we heard this, it was quickly silenced. The enemy regiment was completely destroyed and annihilated. I was told that not one man escaped. Another platoon was coming out from the perimeter to try to help us, and they were redirected to the carnage on the north side of the Oasis for mop-up. We were instructed to proceed back to the perimeter. I was glad. I wanted to rest, and I did not really want to see all the dead. At this point, I had already seen too many dead on both sides. We did clear the Oasis though before we turned back to the perimeter. As my company, now much less than platoon strength, moved up to the enemy regiment CP, we found that our LAWs had taken out both the CP and the mortar positions. This, no doubt, caused the route. There were a lot of dead laying around, and we took wounded prisoners. Most interesting were two dead Russian officers in the CP along with one Chinese officer. These were advisors to the enemy regiment. And we were told there were no Russians. Right! Russia and China played a big role here in this war. Even though we were told they were not participating, we all knew they were, and that the AK47 was a Russian weapon and came directly from Russia to the North Vietnamese Army. I took one of the Russian officer's belts as a souvenir. I did not normally do this, but this time I decided to do it. I still have the belt and a map of the area. I will reprint the map and place it in the index of this book so you can see the area we fought in. I also had picked up the grenade that did not go off, which landed between me and the other Marine. I stuck it in my pack for good luck. I know that was crazy; it could have gone off at any time, but maybe I was a little crazy then. I carried that grenade the rest of my tour in my pack and turned it in when I checked my gear in to return to the United States. That caused a little stir in the rear area where many of the supply Marines had never been in combat and had never even seen an enemy grenade before. They asked if it was live, and I said yes. They all took a little jump and a step back then, and no one wanted to touch it. I just left it on the table and walked away. I heard someone say, "What are we going to do with it?" I figured it probably was live, and the man who put it on the end of the bamboo pole that day on March 9, 1968, to flick it at us just did not turn it enough to activate it before he let it fly. To arm the grenade, you just twisted it. On one end, it had sort of a cone, and the enemy would put that on a bamboo pole and flick it at us, after they twisted it to arm it. They were very good at this technique and could be very accurate. I am sure they practiced.

We now had less than forty men in our company, not enough to even form a full platoon, and the brand-new sergeant was among the dead; so much for a nice stroll in the sun. We walked back to the perimeter and rested. I was very tired. I forgot to get fresh water at the Oasis.

Horst Faas, Associated Press

Chapter 10

Tet Offensive

This really began it all. Until then, things were relatively calm. That is, other than several ambushes that we managed to walk in to like the one with the APC attack. That one was well organized and executed. There were several smaller ones also, on the squad level, when we would do our patrols to determine if the enemy was moving in on our perimeter. They pretty much knew when we would be going out and returning and would try to catch us off guard then. The enemy was good at setting ambushes; I think, better than we were.

I fought in the Tet Offensive, which began on the night of January 30, 1968, a month before the battle of March the sixth. Now the really big battles began. This was the period of time when we lost the most troops in the whole war, and for the enemy, it was all or nothing. At midnight, the dark skies were lit up with explosions and flares. As far as the eye could see, the flashes of orange and red explosions were going off with red traces streaking off in the distance. I have never seen so many explosions all at once. The night sky all around was completely lit up. Not just our perimeter but all around me; at far-off perimeters, it looked like the world was ending and sounded like it. I did not even know some of these perimeters were there before this. This was bad, very bad. A sergeant came running by and said, "Every single perimeter in country is under attack! Da Nang was completely overrun! So, stay down and to shoot anything that moved." He said, "They were already inside our perimeter too, so watch out! Each of you is on his own to survive until morning." Nearly every single base and perimeter in South Vietnam was hit, and many were overrun and captured that night. Da Nang, I felt sorry for them. They considered that base so secure that most Marines did not carry their rifles around with them. Well, I hoped they had them by their bunks that night. Later, I heard many did not. The provincial capital, Hue, fell to the enemy that night, totally overrun and with most of the Marines dead, from what I heard. It would require a week of fighting by the First Marine Division to recover it again. Schwietzer was part of that effort, and that is where he was sentenced to Leavenworth. He wrote to me from Federal Prison telling me about the brutal conditions there in the prison. At the time of his first letter, he was in the prison hospital. He said that one of the guards had thrown him down a flight of stairs after beating him up, and he had a broken leg and arm. I sent him a letter back asking what he did wrong and was hoping I could help him. He sent back a letter saying I could not help. He would be there for twenty years, and then he did the crime. He said that after fierce fighting, his squad had secured the central financial district of the city. He said that they then proceeded to blow down the front door of the largest bank in Hue. They then helped themselves to the money in the bank—very stupid! I was very surprised that such a smart guy could be so stupid, but I guess it was partly the confusion of combat. That can mess up what you're thinking. It is so sad because I thought Schwietzer had so much potential, and to lose it all like this was tragic. He said in his final letter that he did not think he would make it out of Leavenworth alive. I was so sad for him. I never heard from him again and do not know what happened to him. I wish I did. I miss Schwietzer. He did a bad thing, but he was basically a good man.

Our perimeter was also hit by a company of enemy. They hit the north side of our perimeter where I was with my two machine guns. We took lots of incoming with mortars landing near the position I was in. It was necessary for us to move. We moved the gun to the fallback secondary position. We had just left the primary when it was hit by an RPG right through the machine gun opening in the front, which pretty much devastated the bunker. Had we remained a minute longer, we would not have made it. As the assault continued, we were getting low on ammo, so I sent Blake, the ammo humper, to get more from the other gun position. They were not firing their guns as much and did not seem to be getting hit as badly as us. Blake was on his way back when he was hit by a bullet in the back. He was about twenty meters from my position. I crawled out to get him. When I got there, I could see he was not going to make it. I felt bad. He was a good friend and a good Marine. When I got to him, I just sat up, cross-legged, pulled him onto my lap and held him. I was facing the incoming fire from the enemy and could see all the flashes from their weapons in the darkness. Occasionally, there was a red trace following from one of the flashes that would zip by me. I could hear all this rifle fire ripping by me but ignored it. I just concentrated on holding him as he died. I was going to honor my promise, and in a funny way, I was not too concerned about being hit. My men knew what I was doing; they had seen it before. They fired frantically to try and protect me, but the enemy was concentrating on taking me out. Gunfire like crazy. I could see Blake's face in the flashes of the explosions around me and the dull eerie light of the parachute flares. He looked straight into my eyes. He asked in a soft voice, "Am I going to die?" I thought for a second about telling him the truth but decided to say, "Don't worry, you're going to be fine." I did not feel like I was lying. I knew he was going to die very soon in my arms, and I knew he would soon be in heaven, and he would be fine there, taken care of by God. The explosions continued around me, and the bullets whizzed by, but I did not care. I did not care if I was hit; I was going to hold on to Blake until he died. I felt God protected me every time I did this. I prayed to the Holy Ghost for protection on the battlefield and in a lot of things I did. I am not sure why, but he always did answer my prayers, and that is probably why I often prayed to him. I knew I would not be hit, even though I was completely exposed, and the danger was very close and real. I could feel the Holy

Ghost with me and protecting me, and I knew I would not be injured. I held Blake and prayed for him for about fifteen minutes. He groaned a little and called for his mother. I held him closer and told him it would be OK. He smiled slightly at me and was quiet. I could feel him slowly fading away then at the moment of death, I could feel his spirit leave his body and saw in the semidarkness a slight mist lift from his body. I could tell immediately I was holding a dead body, now completely lifeless. I left him then and crawled back to the machine gun position. Things were calming down a bit. I told the team that Blake was dead.

The rest of the battalion was fine. We only took a few casualties on the north of the perimeter. I lost one man, Blake. The rest of the country was in disarray though, and there was heavy fighting everywhere, which continued for the next few days. It appeared that most of the Marine bases held but need reinforcement very badly as many were at the point of collapse. It looked like my battalion was just about the only one in the country at full strength. So, we were called upon to help the others out. I was ready, but I knew it was going to be bad. Our company boarded helicopters the next day, late in the afternoon, and flew off toward one of the distressed perimeters. This was just one of many we would visit over the next few days, and they all needed help. Our company went in one direction. Alpha Company went in another, while Bravo Company held our perimeter. It looked like we had about thirty-five choppers or so. We were flying low over the jungle; it was dramatic seeing us all flying information moving fast to the objective just over the treetops. They stayed low to avoid giving the enemy too much notice before we were on them. This cut down on the Surface to Air Missiles (SAM) that could be fired at us and rifle fire. By the time they were ready to fire, we were gone. I sat in the doorway and looked out over the other choppers flying next to us and at the jungle below. It looked spectacular and like something out of a movie; we looked strong and invincible, and I felt proud to be a part of it, all of us swooping along, flying low to not give the enemy much warning as we passed overhead, toward the east and near the Bay of Tolkien. I could see the jungle reluctantly giving way to sand dunes and sea birds. It was like a whole different world. I watched in amazement as the landscape changed. I suddenly felt uneasy. I was used to fighting in the jungle, not in sand. What would this be like? This was going to be different from what I was used to doing. I wondered if I would be OK. I thought I would make it somehow. My thoughts went back to the coppers and how impressive we looked just above the tree like moving in battle formation. I could see another Marine sitting in the doorway of the chopper flying beside us, and we traded nods. I was thinking that the enemy must be at least a little intimidated when they see us coming in like this. This was my first helicopter assault. I was soon to experience many more assaults like this one over the next few weeks, but this was my first and most exciting of all. In the distance, I could see a perimeter coming into view. It must be the one we were going to help. It looked battered even from this distance. I wondered how many men were left alive and how many they lost. We began to slow a little as we neared their perimeter. I heard a slight ping and saw a ray of light like a laser light appear on the helmet of the Marine next to me; it then started dancing around the helicopter from man to man. It startled me, and I did not know what it was. I looked up and saw a hole in the roof of the chopper, the sun streaming down in a beam to the deck; it looked like a laser light. At first, I did not understand what was happening. I wondered if something dropped on us, then another appeared and another. One of the Marines took off his helmet and sat on it. I still did not get it then looked at the floor and saw the dust coming up and a hole appeared on the deck. Then I realized it was rifle fire from the ground. Other Marines took off their helmets and sat on them. I decided that since I was in the door I would just stay put and hoped I did not get shot in the butt. I was wondering if they were going to land us right in the perimeter or outside to engage the enemy immediately. It turned out that we landed inside; taking turns while the choppers circled above. I was glad when it was our turn to land. I did not enjoy being a target in the air, it was better to be the target on the ground; at least I could look for cover. I felt sorry for the pilots who had to endure this every day. They had absolutely no protection from this kind of stuff and just seemed to ignore it—brave guys! As we got off the choppers, I immediately met one of the "Hawaiians" from my old platoon. It seemed that a lot of them wound up in this unit. I asked him about Magahi and a few others. He told me that during the Tet attack, Magahi was wounded by an enemy mortar, and our gunnery sergeant went out to save him and was carrying him back when they were both killed by another mortar round. I told him about McAllister. It looked like that was pretty much it for the Hawaiians, not too many of us left now. I figured we did not have long left either. McAllister was the last of five Texas sons to die in Vietnam. Before we knew about his brother's deaths, we did not understand why he was so quiet and detached from everyone in boot camp and Infantry Training Regiment (ITR). He was an honor guard in boot camp but did not talk to anyone except to pass along orders. He was a big man and displayed strong leadership skills and a strong mind, a college graduate, which was something unusual for most of us young Marines. Everyone respected him immediately when they met him, but no one understood him. I asked a Marine who seemed to be one of his friends, but he did not know anything either. Most of us out of ITR were sent to Hawaii as our next duty station. I was surprised about me being sent there along with several other two-year guys. Most of the two-year guys went straight to Vietnam so that they could be "utilized" before their two years was up. From what I heard; they did get utilized. With the limited training they had, they did not survive long. I wonder why I was spared and thought it might have something to do with my advanced training and high scores with the M60 machine gun, but I was not sure. By qualifying top in my class, I was given an expert badge in guns and promoted to private first class (PFC). I think I lucked out in the final qualification. This was the toughest part and required firing at a target, fifty meters away, in a standing position, holding the gun up and sighting in like a rifle. The gun is heavy, and I had learned that I needed to lean into it as I fire the three-round burst. Three rounds only, no more, no less, and this in itself took some skill: just the right tap on the trigger. Well, I was lucky, relaxed, and held my breath as in firing the rifle. As I pulled the trigger for the three-round burst, I slightly leaned a little more and a little more forward as each round fire. I could not believe it, three rounds, and dead center, in the bull's-eye. The new Rank had privileges, and the main advantage was that I got off some of what were called "shit details" and often found that I was put in charge of the privates, guys I went through boot and ITR with. This was my first leadership responsibilities. They gave me shit at first as it was difficult to change from being buddies to someone whose orders need to be followed. Life was improving for me though in the Marine Corps. I began to feel like I had made it after being afraid for months that I would fail. Boot camp was very hard for me, and ITR was also a real challenge. At many, many points, I did not think I was going to make it. Magahi had been a very good friend up until now, but this changed. He was really mad that I was giving him orders now. He began to drift away and became good friends with the gunnery sergeant. This was an unlikely friendship as he was only a private, and the "gunny" far out ranked him. One night, Magahi invited me to go with him over to the sergeant's quarters for drinks. I was astounded. I said, "How can you go there? You are not a staff sergeant." He laughed and said, "Oh, the gunny always invites me over." I did not quite believe this, so decided to go along. Sure enough, we were welcomed in; though it was obvious to me the gunny was not super happy to see me there too. Nonetheless, he was polite and offered me a drink too. Well, I had heard the rumors that all the gunny ate was the c-ration cans of fruit cocktail and Wild Turkey whiskey, but now I believed it was true. He opened his footlocker, and all that was in it were bottles of whiskey and fruit cocktail, nothing else. No one had ever seen the gunny in the mess hall. He had his own mess hall in his footlocker. The gunny was skinny as a rail. Everyone loved him and was scared of him, including me. It was said that he had many, many medals for the Korean War, and they joked that he had some from the First World War. The gunny would often come into our barracks on any day but usually on Sunday and proceed to knock out one hundred pushups without stopping or even breathing hard. The gunny was a legend. Our Marine officers would defer to him on military issues just as they would to the first sergeant. The gunny was fifty-five years old I was told, and he had fought in WWII, Korea, and the many miscellaneous wars and expeditions that the Marines had been involved in since WWII. When he wore his ribbons, they filled his blouse, and I'm sure he had to leave some home because they would not all fit. The gunny was highly decorated and highly respected by all and feared by some. I was sorry that both Magahi and the gunny were gone but was glad they could go together. I remembered our nights in Hawaii drinking in the staff sergeant's quarters and knew we would never do that again. Once in a while, I have a glass (or two) of Wild Turkey in memory of the gunny and Magahi. It always makes me sad though.

By my calculations, if I spent a few months in Hawaii, I would not even be able to complete a thirteen-month tour in Vietnam. I wondered if I might not get to Vietnam at all. I was actually a little disappointed because I did want to see combat (well, at least then I did). We spent our time in Hawaii doing advance jungle warfare training and amphibious assault training. We were all given top security clearances and had visits to our families by the FBI. We were told that we were training to be the spearhead assault on Hanoi from the sea. After one of our amphibious training exercises with a practice landing on the Island of Maui, we set sail for a twenty-day trip to the coast of California. This was a long boring trip. I was not used to having time on my hands and not being exhausted. For months I had fallen asleep every night totally exhausted and now had trouble sleeping because I was not tired. This was a new thing for me. We were on troop carriers that must have dated back to World War II. I was deep in the bowls of the ship in a large cabin with one hundred plus Marines stacked like sardines in bunks, eight highs with less than two inches between me and the man above me. The racks were barely six feet long, and we had to keep all our gear with us on the racks. Nothing could be on the deck below as we needed that room to crawl down and assemble to climb over the side of the boat and just like the old-World War II movies; that is exactly what we did. I was carrying the machine gun then as the gunner. It had slept with me for the last twenty days in the tiny bunk and now I was carrying it, tied to my pack, down the side of a troop carrier into the landing craft, which bounced frantically below us in the waves. It was very wavy, and we had waited an extra hour for the seas to calm down a bit before being given the order to go over to the side. I looked down at the navy men in the craft and thought that they looked scared, maybe my imagination, because I was scared. This was tough going down but no sooner had we gotten down, and the assault was canceled. We would not be attacking Camp Pendleton today. We were told to climb back up. I thought someone was crazy. I did not know how we would make it back up with all that weight, but we did. We did except for one man who fell into the churning sea. He had his helmet not strapped on as we had been instructed; otherwise, his head would have been taken off. The helmet went flying back up into the air as he hit. As he hit, he slipped off his pack, which we were also instructed not to wear with more than one release. He did this just as he entered the water, so he did not get sucked down. It was textbook; textbook, that is if you are going to fall off a net on the side of a troop carrier with all your gear on. He was going up, nearly over the rail at the top when he slipped. He went flying right by me. I wanted to reach for him but knew I would go too. It was a long drop into the water, but he was OK. The navy men pulled him from the water.

Another big danger was getting tangled in the net between the large ship and the landing craft as it bobbed about in the waves. Both were heavy enough to easily crush us. The navy men and Marines already down held the nets as taunt as they could to keep this from happening, but with all the bouncing around, it was very hard to do. As I crawled up and over the side of the rail, just barely making it because of all my gear and the gun I was carrying, I happened to glance up at the bridge and saw the captain watching us. I thought I saw a slight grin on his face and a nod of satisfaction as he turned and walked away, but I cannot be sure. He was a long way away. I wondered briefly if this was really just a test of our ability, and there was no plan at all to storm the beaches that day. Don't know. Later we made several landings and held training games at Camp Pendleton for several weeks.

McAllister was with us during the training, and I had a chance to get to know him better. After we did complete our invasion of Southern California, we docked in San Diego for the weekend and were all given liberty.

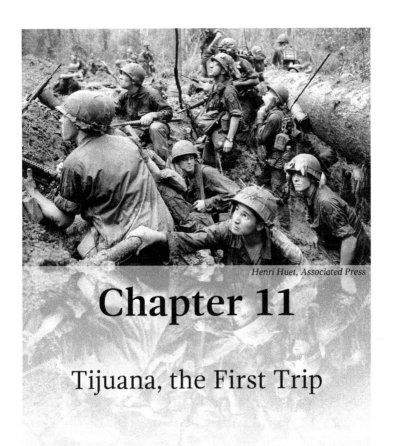

Henri Huet, Associated Press

Chapter 11

Tijuana, the First Trip

We were finally docked in San Diego after our training exercises. We were given liberty. A group of us decided that since we were so close, we would go to Tijuana for the night. We had some fun drinking and raising hell. This was a great opportunity for most of us because we were underage for drinking, and we knew we would get drinks in Mexico but not at most bars in the United States. We talked McAllister into coming with us, although he really did not want to, so the six of us set off by bus to the border. We got there at about 7:00 p.m. on a Friday night, and boy was it wild. We went from bar to bar, taking all the girl shows and drinking like crazy. Some of the things we saw, I could not even have imagined would ever take place. I think the only way to take it all in was to be pretty drunk. I won't go into details here, but just imagine the wildest activities you can think of and that would probably still not do it justice. So, we drank hard, like young Marines who would soon go to war. At about 1:00 a.m., we decided to head back to America and take a cab back to the ship in San Diego. We had carefully set aside enough money for the cab ride back before we began the festivities, so we thought we had everything covered, but then a new wrinkle was added. As we passed over the infamous Tijuana Bridge that leads pretty much to the entrance gates into the United States, we walked past a beer bottle placed on the edge of the brick work at the very top of the curves bridge. McAllister, being in a good mood, just nudged it with his elbow, sending it tumbling to the ground below where it broke into many pieces. Then through our blurred vision, we saw five Mexican police running at us from both sides of the bridge. They had us trapped. We fell for the "set-up." One pointed at McAllister, and two police grabbed him, while the rest stood defensively as if expecting an attack from the rest of us. We did not, of course, knowing that we already had enough trouble—pretty good I thought for a bunch of drunken Marines. We caught a cab and went to the jailhouse where they were holding McAllister. We asked the Mexican sergeant what we could do to get him out because the ship sailed at 6:00 a.m., just about five hours from then. We did not want to leave McAllister behind; we were the ones who told him in to come with us. The sergeant indicated it would be $500 to get him free. We formulated a plan; take a cab back to the ship, wake everyone up and get money for his bail and the trip both ways in the cab and bring him home. We knew it would be very close, and that we might not make it in time, and all might miss the boat and be AWOL, but we had to do it. We did. We did not all have to go back to get him, but everyone wanted to, even though it was a big risk. When we got to the jail, the price had gone up to $600, but we had enough extra—we got him in the cab and headed back to the United States, San Diego, and our now so appealing ship. We asked the driver to go like hell, and he did, as best he could without getting in trouble. We came running up the gang plank at exactly 6:00 a.m., saluted the flag and the bridge, and ran to our quarters. My sergeant said he did not think we were going to make it but was glad we did. McAllister would not go out with us again (no surprise there, but we still asked him) and made sure he paid every penny back to everyone who helped.

The enemy had surrounded this perimeter where we had just landed and was about to destroy it. We did not hesitate though. Once all the men were unloaded, we walked straight out through the front gate to meet the enemy. It was late. The sun was about to set, and I knew we would be out there in the dark soon. We walked out about one hundred meters, to a point just in front of the jungle and were told to hold up and settle into the dry rice paddy fields for the night. We did not get fired on, but I knew they were just in front of us in the jungle, watching us. I could feel the eyes on us and was wondering why they did not open up. I thought that maybe they were just waiting to see what we would do for the night and if we would come into the jungle. I thought it was strange that we were ordered to stop in the open like that with only the short rice paddy dykes as cover.

I did not like it but did not question orders; there were usually good reasons for orders like this. I did think though that we would be sitting ducks there, and we were, and that is exactly what the company commander wanted. We were bait; now to catch some fish.

I did something very stupid, and this was the only time I did it in Vietnam. I did not dig a fox hole for the night. For some reason, I decided I would be OK behind the dyke, and that I did not need a hole that night. I just took off my cartridge belt and laid it next to me. Put my rifle on top of me, making sure safety was off and ready to fire, and fell to sleep. It was the first full night of sleep I got since entering Vietnam, well sort of, I slept off and on, standing my own watch partially through the night as I was concerned that they might sneak in out of the jungle just in front of us; always before we were two to a hole with alternating watches, so the most sleep was three hours at a time. Just at dawn, the firing started. The enemy was all over the front of the tree line, and we were taking intense fire. We were completely pinned down—just where we wanted them! We were looking for a pitch battle, here and now. The tree line was very close, around fifteen meters (ninety feet) away. I decided to poke my head up to take a look and to see if I could get a shot at one of the enemies. A bullet immediately hit the bank right in front of my face tossing up dirt into my eyes. I put my head down. They had my position now; I was in trouble. Rounds, lots of rounds, were hitting the dyke in front of me, and some were landing all around me. I put my rifle over the dyke to fire but keeping my head behind the dyke, getting off two rounds before a round pinged of the barrel nearly knocking the rifle out of my hands. I knew I had to roll out of there fast. I did, grabbing my cartridge belt as I went. I only rolled twice then laid there looking at the area I had just vacated. It was covered, every square inch, by bullets. I would have been riddled if I had stayed there a moment longer. The fire from the jungle seemed to intensify like a swarm of bees. It felt like they were getting ready for the attack and to wipe us out. I could not put my head up, so again I stuck my rifle over the top of the bank and fired. I grabbed a grenade and lobbed it into the jungle, then another. I saw one of the men from weapons platoon standing with a bazooka. He was the last Hawaiian other than me left in our company. I did not know him very well, but he was a good guy. I could not believe he was standing and trying to fire the bazooka, and he was taking his time. Now we all fired and fired hard to protect him as much as we could, but still the enemy concentrated on him with bullets landing all around him. Since they were all aiming at him, I was able to sit up and take some good shots where I saw flashes from the rifle fire coming from the trees. I thought that at any second he would fall. I do not know how he could possibly remain standing. After what seemed an eternity, he fired. He did not fire far, just right in front of us in the jungle. I expected a big explosion, but there was none, just red smoke coming from the ground. I was beginning to understand what was going on. The red smoke was used to mark an enemy position. Next all the infantry men reached in their packs and put out yellow flags about ten inches square and laid them on the dyke in front of them. I did not even know they carried these. Next, they came screaming in at super high speed and very low to the ground, two Marine jets. Napalm! I saw the big barrels released from the underside of the jets. They were so close I thought I could reach out and touch them. I was about to learn the meaning of close air support, very close. It was so close the heat felt like it was burning the back of my legs and butt. I felt like I could reach out and touch the flames. They circled and came back again. More napalm. I felt sorry for the enemy. It must have been a terrible death. It was right on top of them. I did not see how any could possibly make it out alive. The firing from the enemy had stopped after the first napalm drop. They had fallen for the trap that I did not even know was under way. The Marine jets came again this time with HEAT, dropping the bombs right in front of us. The explosions lifted me up off the ground several inches. I heard it come in and slam into the ground and then felt the searing heat from the shrapnel as a large sharp chunk slammed down sticking point down into the ground right between my legs. It was practically touching my balls with less than an inch to spare. I could feel the red heat from it on my private parts. I rolled again and looked at it, and it was still glowing red hot. I thought, well, at least it would have cauterized the wound as it cut in. That was close I thought. Now I was hoping they would not come back again, but they did, for several more runs. I just hung on hoping no more shrapnel would come my way and mad at myself for not having dug a fox hole. I swore that would never happen again, no matter how tired I was, or how safe I thought it was. I did dig in every time after that.

They came in for one last pass firing their machine guns into the area. I wondered why. Nothing could be possible be left alive in there, but there was. Not only was at least one left alive, but he opened up with a machine gun directly at the incoming jets. I could not believe it, and even more astounding, he hit one of them. The jet started spewing smoke from one of its engines and visibly lost power. It looked like he was going to be OK though, and I heard later he made it back to the aircraft carrier just off the coast from us. Well, now we would take care of that enemy left alive through all of that. I still cannot believe he survived all of that bombing and napalm. The Corporal who fired the bazooka made a bee line for where I was laying before we began to move on the decimated tree line. He was grinning from ear to ear, well not quite from ear to ear because his right ear was missing. It was shot off during the firing of the bazooka. Blood was still dripping from the bandage. He very proudly showed me a bullet hole in his flak jacket and a bullet hole that went right though one of his canteens. This guy was lucky. I told him, "Good job!" and shook his hand. He got the bronze star for that plus the Purple Heart for his wound from what I heard. I think he deserved it.

We did move in on the enemy who had shot our Marine jet. He put up a battle and wounded two more Marines before we got him, but we did get him. He was a staff sergeant and a brave one and fought to the end. I had to respect this enemy soldier. He stayed until he was killed. He was all alone, and none of his other men will ever know how courageous he was, fighting right up until the end. I thought that he must have known he was going to die, that this was his day to die. I wonder what he was feeling—fear, satisfaction, pain, anger, sadness—maybe all these things? I was not happy that he hurt so many Marines, but nonetheless I respected him and thought he was a very honorable man and good at what he did. I was happy that now he would not be able to shoot any more of us. I was happy that we took out such a strong enemy. There is no doubt in my mind that he had killed many of us before this day. It seems true to me that in war, just a relative few do most of the killing, while the rest just seem to go through the motions. He was one of those that did most of the killing.

We then went after the rest of them, scattered through the jungle, around the perimeter. As I moved with my new squad through a field toward a tree line about five hundred meters in front of us, the man on my right, about three meters away, crumpled to the ground. A second or so later I heard the shot from the enemy rifle. This meant he was shot from a long way away. Was this a sniper? I had never heard of an NVA sniper and did not know they had them. As I mentioned, most of them were bad shots. I took a closer look at the downed Marine, and he had a bullet right between his eyes. I looked at the men, and before I could say anything, I saw another man's helmet fly off and the blood spurting from the back of the head, another hit right between the eyes! I yelled at the rest of the men that it was a sniper, to get down, keep their heads down, and not look up. I said, "If you look up and try to see where he is, you will be shot between the eyes. This guy is very, very good and can hit us in the head at over a mile away!" I sent a man to crawl back to the lieutenant and let him know we had a very good sniper in the tree line in front of us, and we had two dead already. The company came to a stop, while the lieutenant tried to call in artillery on the tree line in front of us. It took more than an hour, but we did finally get the support. They were able to blast the tree line. I doubt we got the sniper because by the time the artillery hit it, I thought he was long gone. Well, at least he was not a problem after that, so maybe we got him. I felt bad that I lost two more of my Marines, both good friends. It seemed such a waste of life. I think it was at that point that I began to withdraw from social contact with my men. Up until then, I had been involved with their lives, gotten to know them, and heard stories about their families, their brother and sisters, their parents, where they grew up, where they went to school, what they did at school, their cars, girlfriends, but suddenly I did not want to know anymore. It just hurt too much when they would die. I guess this is when I stopped eating too. I did not even realize I had stopped eating, but a couple days later, one of my men gave me a chocolate coconut bar from the c-rations. This was one of the more coveted treats in the c-rations (that is, next to the fruit cocktail). I took it and took a couple bites and then started to put it away, to save for later. The Marines said I should finish it. I said, "I am not very hungry. I will eat it later." Later another man in my squad brought me a can of peaches (third most coveted, then again, probably number 1). Now, this was truly the most relished treat in the c-rations. It was sweet, tasted great, and helped quench the thirst. I thought something was up here. We do not just give the best away, maybe a bargain for something else, but not give away. I asked, "Why are you guys giving me the good stuff?" He said, "Well, Corporal, we are worried about you. You are not eating." I said, "What do you mean? I eat all the time." He said, "When was the last time you had a meal? We have been watching you, and when we break and have a meal, you just drink some water, nothing else." I said, "No. I have been eating." He said, "Think about it. Did you have lunch today? Did you have anything for breakfast and what about supper last night?" I thought and realized suddenly he was right. I was very skinny now and thought briefly, *how I can be so skinny and carry all of this weight.* I realized it was getting harder and harder to carry the weight and move through the jungle. I needed to start eating. He said, "You have not had anything to eat for a couple days now. You've got to eat." I promised him I would and got out some c-rations and really did make an attempt to eat. For some reason, it was difficult. I too knew that if I did not eat, I would not be able to continue. I started to force myself to eat at every meal, but I was not hungry. I had to talk myself into eating each time, even though I did not feel like it. I thought about it and realized I saw this happen to other NCOs toward the end of their tours. They just seemed to sort of start giving up. I was not going to let this happen to me though. I was finally able to overcome this problem and did start to eat more but could not get myself to socialize much with the men. I knew I should but could not. I had just seen too many of them die, and it was very painful every time. I remembered my NCO (actually my second one) when I first got to Nam and before I became the NCO. The Corporal was cleaning his pistol, and it went off putting a bullet right into his stomach. My fox hole was right next to his, and when the gun went off, I really jumped, since it was inside the wire and not coming from outside. The corpsmen treated him for about an hour to control the bleeding before they got him on a chopper. It was a very bad wound, and they did not know if he would live. I heard a lot of speculation that it might not have been an accident. The men were saying that he never talked to anyone anymore and had completely withdrawn. I tended to believe that it was not an accident. One thing we know as Marines is how to handle weapons, and the first thing we do when we clean a weapon is to make sure it is not loaded. This would have amounted to a rookie mistake, and that Corporal was anything but a rookie. I do think it was a Marine who had given up hope. I prayed that he would make it and be OK, but I knew that even if he did not die from the wound, he would carry these scars the rest of his life. We all would. I did not understand all of this at that time and even was critical of the Corporal for letting him go. I thought about him a lot and could not understand how he could do this, but then, one day, I understood, and I was him. I mean, I would not do that, but I understand how it would be possible, after seeing enough of the war, after enough killing and death.

US Army: Public Domain

Chapter 12

The Helicopter

We continued to "mop up" the enemy around the perimeter until the threat was pretty much removed. We then moved onto another perimeter, which had pretty much the same situation. They were ready to be overrun with only a small contingent of Marines still alive. On the next one, we assaulted right into the enemy from the helicopters. It was a firefight from the beginning to the end. We had close air support, very close, from the Marine pilots. This helped a lot and was probably the only reason we were beating the enemy back. Without the jets, it would have just been a slugging match, trading one bullet round for another. The enemy had real fear of our jets. I would have too. They screamed in and dealt death from the sky. There was no time to run and no place to get to for safety. The enemy was doomed if they were in the sites of a Marine jet pilot. Either they would be shot up by the heavy machine gunfire, napalmed, or blown up by "heat" rounds. Any of these methods meant certain death. From the events of the day and the fierce fighting though the jungle, across streams, from bomb crater to bomb crater, we had quite a few wounded and dead. Because of all the other activity going on in Vietnam with many battles still going on after the Tet Offensive, we had trouble getting in medevac coppers. So as night approached, we had the wounded and dead Marines line up in the center of the perimeter awaiting evacuation. We had again lost a lot of corpsmen, but those that were left attended to our wounded. Before dark I noticed that they were lined up in order, with the most critical at the front of the line on down to the rows of dead. It got dark and still no coppers. I was worried; some of those men would be dead by morning. I knew choppers did not fly at night very often, and on such a busy day, I did not expect to see any until dawn, if even then. It was just about 1:00 a.m., and I heard it. There was a chopper headed in our direction. I was in my fox hole about fifty meters from LZ. I was very relieved. Someone was coming in to get our men, someone very brave to be flying in and in the middle of the night in a heavy combat area. I heard the chopper stop and hover over the LZ. He held his position for about a minute. He was drawing some small arms fire from the enemy, which our men responded to. Suddenly, he turned on his powerful spotlight and lit up the area. I thought either this guy is very brave or crazy, or both. He still hovered, now taking more fire since his position was easily determined. I looked at the LZ but saw no one there to guide him into the landing. I was not too surprised; it was a very exposed position. Someone needed to get out there and guide him down, but I saw no one going, and the chopper just hovered, exposed to all the fire. I stood and ran to the LZ, placing myself at the head of the chopper and moving him down. I felt very exposed, standing in the middle of the LZ with the bright light on me, and thought that I might, at any second, be one of those wounded or dead lying at the edge of the LZ, and join them, to be loaded on this very chopper; as one more casualty. Fire whined past my head. The bullets were close; I wanted to duck, to lay flat on the ground as I always did when I was being shot at, but I knew this had to be done. I was very afraid but put it aside and ignored the fear. This had to be done; I had to stand, even if I died in this very spot.

The chopper came to a gently landing, and the pilot turned off the bright spotlight. I was relieved by that. I began immediately to load the wounded at the head of the line; some corpsmen and Marines appeared to help me. I noticed all the blood on the deck of the chopper (this chopper had been busy today); also, there was no door machine gunner (the gun hung nose down, limp as if having been shot itself; I pictured the gunner falling as he was hit), and the crew sergeant was not on board. I saw a pile of bloody flak jackets lying against the bulkhead. I guessed the pilots lost both crew members on earlier missions that day.

We had all of the seriously wounded on board, and I was thinking about a few more but knew that we were near lifting capacity and heavy loads was an issue with these choppers. I looked up to the pilot for some direction, hoping he would indicate I could add a few more of the less critical men. The pilot was watching me and just gave me a "thumbs up." I took that to mean that we were good for now. I gave him a "thumbs up" back and then noticed the copilot slumped over, blood dripping from his helmet, adding to that already on the deck and the additional added by my men. I was stunned. This pilot had come in alone, in the middle of the night, to help us. I stepped off the running blade of the chopper and ran back to my fox hole. I heard him power up his engine, lift, and pull away, heading toward Da Nang. I was very grateful for the pilot, a great man. He saved many lives that night by risking his own life and coming into a "hot" LZ. I knew he didn't have to. I knew men would die if he had not. God bless him. God bless them all but especially him!

US Army. Public Domain

Chapter 13

Replacements

By now, our company and the two others had been reinforced by primarily raw Marines straight from boot camp and actually not too many of them. We usually ran at about half the men we really should have had to fill out a squad. This, of course, made it a lot more difficult to carry equipment and the ammo for guns. The extra weight made our jobs more difficult, but we had to carry the ammo just in case we needed it (and we usually did). I had been busy training my two machine gun teams as most of the men were not 0331 MOS. In fact, I was the only one actually trained with guns. I taught them how to break down and clean the guns, how to clear jams, how to establish fields of fire, how to overlap fire at the most likely point of advance and attack, how to establish secondary fallback positions, how to carry and conceal the gun, how to keep the bullets clean, how to setup for night fire, how to practice fire control and not give away our positions, how to work with the rest of the platoon and position among the riflemen, how to fire the gun both in a position, when advancing on the enemy and in the standing rifle position, what the job of the gunner was, what the job of the A-gunner was, what the job of the first and second ammo humper was, when not to fire, when to fire (our guns [as theirs were] were major targets for the enemy; we need to use them, but we needed to protect them), ammo control, evaluation of enemy strength, defensive strategy, offensive strategy with gun, going on patrols, going on search and destroy. A long list and there were many other details such as mounting the gun on the tripod, when to do it and when not to do it. Also, changing the barrel of the machine gun; when it overheated because of excessive firing, which was pretty easy and quick but, in the middle of a battle, the A-gunner would often forget to put on the asbestos glove and would burn his hand. These barrels could get red hot and would actually bend after excessive firing, so they needed to be exchanged with the spare barrel to let them cool off. I heard of men peeing on the barrel to cool it down, but I wondered who would stand up during the middle of an attack to do that. Usually, there were too many bullets flying in at the gun. Throwing some canteen water on it might be an option, but usually we were low on water or out of it.

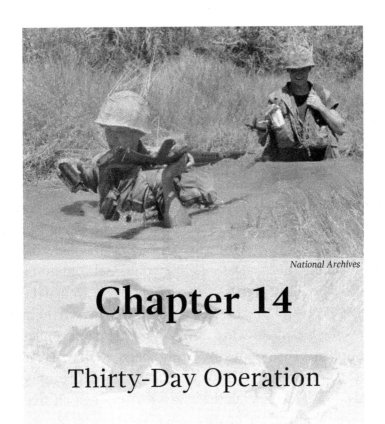

National Archives

Chapter 14

Thirty-Day Operation

We were to begin a thirty-day operation, and we were told that we would never stay a second night in the same place. This would involve the whole battalion, three full companies, plus some support unit such as snipers, totaling just about one thousand men, a very large force to be going through the dense jungle. The idea was that if we made contact with even a whole division of north regulars, we would be able to handle the situation, and making contact with a division of enemy was exactly what we were looking for. They told me we would be moving through thick jungle. We would be moving in areas suspected to be stronghold of the enemy. We would move without helicopter support, so that the enemy did not know we were coming. What they told us was correct. We went into dense jungle forded streams filled with leeches and continually faced climbs up steep hills and then down the other side. During on-stream crossing, I got six leeches attached to me, sucking my blood. I did not even know they were there at first. I heard the Marine behind me cursing and saw him frantically peeling of his clothes just after we got to the other side of the chest high stream. I took a step back to see what was going on and saw two big leeches hanging from his chest. My first thought was, poor guy, sure glad I did not get any on me (because I thought I would feel something like that—looked pretty gross), then I thought, well if he got them right behind me then I should probably have them too. I saw some blood showing through my leg pants, pulled the cloth up, and sure enough, a large leech is attached to my right calf. While half of the squad stood guard, the other half pulled off all of their clothes. We had leeches all over us. They were big and fat, engorged with our blood. We got out the "bug juice." Spraying a little bug juice on them usually made them pull their heads out of our skin. You do not want to just pull them off because the head would stay in your skin and become infected and then could lead to much more serious problems. Most of the six were on my legs, but one was on my arm, and another was on my private part. I got them all off with the bug juice, but the one on my privates really stung a lot. Hated leeches and it was amazing how much blood they could suck up in just a few minutes.

For those of us that were left and had survived the battle of March the 6th the war continued on and became more deadly. We continued to fight on, however, hoping and praying for survival. The battles were fierce. I was certain I would not make it but somehow, I did. I did survive and then began the battle to not lose my sanity.

Printed in the USA
CPSIA information can be obtained
at www.ICGtesting.com
LVHW070624260923
759106LV00003B/461

9 781961 123410